Bok Choy's Bike Ride

By Jenell Nyberg

CONTENTS

Dedication

This book is dedicated to four special people in my life.

Betty Porter, who believed in me.

Allison Israel, who always encouraged me.

And Sandra Nyberg and Samson York, who hold my heart.

Introduction

I was bicycling through the town of Dushore, Pennsylvania, population 640 when my intuition told me that today I was going to die. Every cell in my body resonated with "lay down and die!"

The truth was that by the time I had found myself in upstate New York, I was already dying.

For three days I had been soaking wet, trapped in my tent, shivering from hypothermia, and developing a deep and nagging cough.

A cough that would later translate into pneumonia. In case you do not know, it is very difficult to ride your bike in the mountains when you have pneumonia.

Recalling the wisdom from "Tony"- the bike tourist from Queens I hooked up with after my ride in Iowa, there are two types of people who bike tour:

"Those with all the right gear and know-how, and those with all the gumption." I, apparently, was the latter

Gumption alone was not going to get me out of this mess. This mess of deliberately taking shallower and shallower breaths as the days wore on since finding myself trapped in that rainstorm because once I started coughing, I couldn't stop.

Really trying not to cough when I ate or drank, because the coughing would be so violent and unstoppable it would make me throw-up.

Of course, the exact moment of my cellular exclamation, as I may refer to how my body was screaming at me, happened precisely as I was passing by the local medical clinic in Dushore, PA. And so, as anyone as in touch with his or her intuition and body as I am would do, I stopped in the office and collapsed on the floor.

“What’s wrong?!” the nurse who rushed into the entrance to tend to me asked me.

“I think I’m dying” was all I could get out.

Oh, how good it felt to feel the carpet on my face. Just to be lying down. I was ready to go. I didn’t have any more fight left in me. First, it was my heart, long before I even pushed one pedal of my bicycle on the pavement. Then it was my spirit, somewhere amid the blistering heat on an Illinois highway with no shoulder and a broken spoke. But now, finally, it was my body. I was ready to surrender.

This is where God met me with the first undeniable expression of supernatural provision in my life. My story is one of wild rebellion met with grace and provision that has no explanation in reason or logic. It is so audacious and rich that it must be cosmic.

I come to you, fifteen years after this bike ride, with a simple message. I hope you can hear me when I tell you. That exactly where you are on your journey, with all its grit and pain and potholes and broken spokes, is exactly where Love wants to meet you. That you’re perfect. You are fully lovable right now. There is perfect love, grace, and provision waiting for you. Right now.

Just by reading this introduction, my dream is for you to know that is how at least one person sees you. I hope that in sharing my story of pain and redemption, you may find your own story of hope and healing as we sojourn together in this magnificent human experiment.

Yours,

Jenell

Part 1
Becoming Bok Choy

If you don't know the backstory of my life leading up to my epic, $10 bicycle ride across the US and Canada, most certainly the title of this book has already left you with questions. Who is this "Bok Choy" and how can an Asian cabbage ride a bike? I'm glad you asked. Without going into all the details about my college experience, when I was 20, after my junior year at the University of Iowa, I dropped out of college and moved to an "intentional community" in Virginia. This is a fancy term for what you may more commonly understand as a commune. As you will discover about me, when I go for something I tend to go all in. Head first. And with a splash. So if I was going to drop out of college, I might as well drop out of society while I'm at it. It was only logical, I thought.

I have a somewhat unique trait that affords me comfortability with a very specific risk. For most of my life, risk of the known has generally been perceived as significantly greater than the risk of the unknown. This is why staying in one place terrified me for so long. And still does to some extent. Why I feel and itch to sell all my possessions and move nearly every spring. Why getting comfortable scares me. My biggest fear is complacency. The thought of it sneaking into my life and finding a home scares the friggin' crap out of me. So when school and life seemed to be asking me to make commitments, and to maybe get comfortable settling into something I knew for the long haul, I packed my life in a backpack and left a place that felt safer for me. The unknown.

And that unknown was Twin Oaks Community, one of the oldest "intentional communities" in North America. This book is not about Twin Oaks and my time there. But I will spend a little bit of time there for a number of reasons. For one, it was there that Bok Choy was born. The name was my first attempt to make sense of my place in a world unlike any I had ever known, where I was not quite sure of the rules.

My way is a playful way, so when I learned that most people at Twin Oaks changed their name to their "Spirit Vegetable" or some crap like that, I picked the silliest name I could think of in an attempt to join the club without taking myself, or their little anarcho-communal socialist experiment, too seriously. I thought I was in good company, amid the Radishes and Turnips, Rivers and Sky Blues.

So yes, Twin Oaks was the birthplace of Bok Choy, an identity I carried all through my twenties and therefore during my bike ride I would take four years after "joining the club" (or dare I say, cult?). But it was also much more than that. It was a place of great pain, love, and trauma, and ultimately a scene of crisis for me at a juncture in my life which was more tender than I could have realized at the time.

In my youthful arrogance and naivete, I simply believed I could do anything and have anything I wanted. More accurately, I felt entitled to do anything and have anything I wanted. This sense of entitlement had left my heart still hemorrhaging with pain from a lost love the previous summer and a bitter rejection of "second best" when I couldn't go to school the way I wanted to. I was painfully resentful of forces outside my control. School. Math itself. My dad. Unrequited love. Divorce.

In what I considered to be a most magnificent "Fuck You" to everything I couldn't control, I completely abandoned my life and the path I seemed to be on. It's hard to explain how math has come to take over my life. Math has always been my first love and certainly my safest place. The place to escape and find beauty and intrigue, mysteries longing to be solved. Patterns as old as the ages, begging to be seen in a new light. Symmetry. The simplest symmetry gave me great comfort. In this world, I was never alone. I could sit with the spiral in a pinecone and know that Fibonacci was ever near. Feeling the pull of perfect elliptical curves from the heavens would draw my heart to a space of awe.

But then things like the Incompleteness Theorem crept in, and uncertainty and garbage seemed to find their way into my sacred space. Everything I had learned to trust and find comfort in seemed to vanish. My world stopped feeling ordered and filled with beauty. My mom and dad were getting divorced. The boy I loved was far away from me. I had planned to move to Budapest, Hungary for my senior year and immerse myself in a world of number theory and maybe never come back. But that plan was abruptly stolen from me as well.

The National Science Foundation kept giving me money to solve math problems. So, while working on my math assignment after junior year, I waited for my escape to present itself. While finishing up the summer I happened to make friends with some college students at the nearby Quaker college. I was crashing on their couch and I woke in the middle of the night with my hand on a book that was on the floor. It was entitled Is It Utopia Yet? by Kat Kinkade, one of the founders of Twin Oaks. I read it in a haze from 1 am to 5 am. I was delirious. I sat up and said to myself, "It is my destiny to go to Twin Oaks."

In all reality, I was far too easily influenced, in part by my lack of sleep as well as my desperation to find something that I could fall into that would allow me to forget all the pain I was trying to avoid facing. I couldn't go back to life as I knew it. I simply couldn't bear it. And so, in this way, the risk of the known outweighed the risk of the unknown.

I got up, went to a computer, and wrote a letter to the Twin Oaks membership liaison and poured out my heart. About why it was my destiny to go to Twin Oaks. About how I was a hard worker from the midwest (a huge selling point in my letter, I would later learn, because Twin Oaks essentially functioned as a work camp). About how, in my five-year plan, I hoped to find myself in India scrubbing elephants. What a strange thing to include, yet I carried a torn page from National Geographic with me in my wallet displaying this ritual. I was a girl hungry for adventure. I thought I would be able to find it while married to Mathematics, but now it was time to let that go.

LSD, Rape, and a Stolen $4000

I arrived in Virginia by train with nothing more than a backpack and the clothes on my back, which consisted of Earth Shoes and a beautiful skirt from India. I was greeted by two older hippies dressed in worn-out out and ragged clothing. I wouldn't really realize how impoverished our collective lifestyle would become until I was fully entangled in it and then entirely unable to see clearly. How we wouldn't have new things, like underwear. Or bourgeois luxuries like fresh fruit and store-bought toothpaste. Seeing these two communards, off the farm, they were clearly out of place. But they were kind and friendly, and I soon secretly developed a quiet crush on the guy, who was sort of dorky and cute, even if he was a little older.

I participated in the visitor program, left and traveled to New York City, and finally returned as a provisional member on Halloween night. I arrived at their main building where a raging party unlike anything I had ever witnessed was going on. I was a bit freaked out. At the time, the richest and most charismatic man at Twin Oaks found me standing outside the threshold to the party, placed his hands on my shoulders from behind, and whispered in my ear "Welcome to Paradise."

I recognized him from my time as a visitor. He was carrying his four-year-old son on his shoulders. He asked me if I would like any party favors. And this is where our tale gets a bit strange. Though no one will believe that I was this naive, I truly did not know that the little paper he ripped for me in the walk-in cooler and placed on my tongue was LSD. When we exited the cooler, Mr. Charisma showed me to a man I had met during my time traveling after the visitor program. He was wearing white gloves and dancing in a total trance. He told me if I needed anything, to just find the white gloves. And the person wearing them would take care of me.

The party faded and so did I. I was exhausted from raging on the LSD and the man with white gloves found me and asked me if I would like to go to the treehouse. I agreed and took a long trek into the woods to a magical treehouse where my innocence would be brutally torn and destroyed amid a silent forest. I recall later how I had betrayed the wisdom of my mother, who had once warned me, "Never go into the woods with a man alone." As a young girl I didn't understand why she would give me such a strange warning. Now, with the sun rising and my mind still recovering from drugs and assault, blood streaks on my inner thighs, my psyche was completely fragmented. I dragged my sleeping bag out of the woods, through the fields, past the dairy cows, and found my room.

Something happened over the next two weeks in that hell of a red room. A pain opened up as a perfect slit on my lower left abdomen and I became delirious. I couldn't eat. And I could barely sleep due to the intensity of the pain. To pass the time, I stared at my ceiling and watched a spinning wheel pace above me as if on a track. It became clear to me why I was here. It was my manifest destiny to experience all the pain possible in the universe through a tiny, three-inch slit in my side.

During those two weeks, I was taken to the emergency room twice. The young, southern MD's straight out of medical school could not pinpoint what was wrong with me. It was a different time, and so I was just sent home with opioids for the pain. Of course, news about any drug travels fast at a place like Twin Oaks, and my medicine was strategically stolen from my room to be used recreationally.

But there was also another dynamic coming into play during my time of illness. The man with the white gloves, who lived seven miles away in a neighboring community, began walking the dirt and gravel path every night to spoon feed me yogurt, one of the foods available that I could tolerate. It was a very confusing experience. And my mind began to close and shut away the details of what had happened that night at the party and in the treehouse.

After three weeks of convalescing in my red room, I decided that I had made a mistake coming to Twin Oaks. I still had quite a bit of money left over from my summer research grant, so I decided to buy a train ticket and head back home, with home being my father's house and childhood home in central Iowa. But as I attempted to pay for my ticket, my beat up little debit card kept getting declined. Finally, I called my bank and discovered that my account had exactly $0 in it.

My father had helped me open my checking account when I was fourteen, and so he was joint on the account. I didn't know all the details of what was going on, just that he was going through a divorce and bankruptcy, but he had clearly taken out all of my cash, roughly around $4000. I was beginning to gain my strength back after three weeks stuck in bed. As the sun poured through my window one morning, I decided that I had made my bed here at Twin Oaks, and now it was time to lie in it. So I got up, and began to participate in life in the community.

One of the first things I was met with was hostility over choosing the name "Bok Choy." While shoveling compost out of a heavy, rusted wheelbarrow during a garden shift, a woman with the name of a common household fruit told me that she didn't like my chosen namesake, because she felt like I was making fun of her, and that she liked her name. I couldn't really argue with her feelings, because they were in fact quite valid. I thought she did sound stupid. I thought everyone sounded like idiots around here. The truth was, I was pretty angry with what I was experiencing and didn't quite know how to channel it.

Meanwhile, the man with the white gloves decided to move to Twin Oaks. He did a visitor program. And then he moved into a bedroom right next to mine. It was truly horrible, because he gave me so much attention and everyone in the community seemed to agree that he should be my boyfriend. I really didn't care for him all that much, but I couldn't deny that he had "helped" me while I was sick and I was really overwhelmed with the amount of attention he put into convincing me to "agree" to a relationship I did not want.

I was still intrigued by the cute, older man who had picked me up from the train, but even that wasn't much more than an intrigue and mild crush. There were so many insane sexual expectations placed upon the younger women at Twin Oaks. There was so much pressure to be in a relationship, or several, and every mild flirtatious exchange seemed to have a sexual expectation and then demand associated with it.

I would end up kind of pulling an "Andy Warhol" on the community. On the entire system. I would find a way to play by the rules while saying "Fuck You!" to the whole structure, and then take any and everything I wanted. Well, that is not entirely true. There was really only one thing I still wanted. Something I was coming to terms with that I would never have but still grieved my bruised little heart. Thanksgiving was coming up, and it would mark the one year anniversary of the last time I had seen the boy I had given my heart to in what felt like an entire lifetime ago. The boy who seemed to be compromising his soul for a PhD in mathematics, immersed in a world of topology, while eating nothing but rice and tea. The boy who still never had a bike his whole life.

The boy I would desperately plan to see, then avoid entirely, on my bike ride because I couldn't bear to face him five years later after all I had been through. Maybe he remembered me as a virginal hippie girl with long hair and a faded green dress, with some kind of unique aptitude for math who couldn't be counted on to stay in one place long enough to see it through. Who maybe was too much like wind. Who talked too fast and commanded a presence of unpredictability and mirth. Who seemed liable to latch on to any whim with recklessness and love without agenda or refinement. Who still met love without shame.

Hacking the Labor System

The nuances of the labor system at Twin Oaks were complex, to say the least. I doubt my ability to relay to a lay person exactly how it worked and how I was able to essentially generate labor credits in the absence of work. To my readers familiar with the labor system, I will simply state: I took over quota credits in the same weeks I accrued personal service credits. Since both of these forms of labor were mostly unregulated, the combination and the way I navigated selling wine for personal service credits and then the way I "approved" all my overquota in the department I managed, which was mushrooms, allowed me to generate unlimited, unregulated labor.

How I discovered this logical loophole first came about quite innocently. I simply had a week where I legitimately earned quite a bit of personal service credits, and I asked the labor manager if I would be allowed to claim over quota. He simply said "yes."

I have a mind which processes systems through logic. It simply was my conditioning. In math, when you discover a new world, you first identify the axioms, or rules, then explore the implications of those axioms within the system. After thinking about what I had just discovered, when I truly realized the implication of this lack of restriction on our labor system when taken to their most extreme, I finally had my big "Fuck You." I was off the labor system, essentially independently wealthy. With my new "hack," I could get labor credit doing whatever I wanted, not necessarily what the community "valued" through the traditional labor restrictions. This included hula hooping, playing my whistle, tripping on magic mushrooms, and making wine.

I made it my public mission to mock the labor system that everyone else seemed so controlled and ruled by. I did it in a joking spirit, which carried both a playful and abrasive side simultaneously. To me it was all just part of the experiment. What are the rules of the system, and what happens when you play (or don't play) by the rules? I made a point of playing by the formal rules to the T, but breaking every norm and unspoken expectation with a brashness that simply could not go unnoticed.

I especially liked to mess with the garden laborers, because their work was particularly righteous and the manager of that department held an exceptional disregard, and then eventually outright contempt, toward me. I might pop a huge pot of popcorn and then share it with them, reminding them that if I fed seven people, my time would be labor creditable.

Or I might spend all night baking brownies with peanut-butter filling, cutting them thick and freezing them, and then offering them freely to all the exhausted, hot, and hungry workers in the middle of the field. Just to see what would happen. To see who would be pissed and who wouldn't be.

My game and experiment got especially interesting when I decided to run for highest office at the community. I once again saw an interesting potential in the political environment. Given that three candidates appeared to be drawing upon the same pool of supporters, I saw that I may in fact have a chance at election if they "Ralph Nadered" each other out. I rallied on an extreme political platform and mocked the system entirely. I adapted my wine labels for political ads and wrote any slogan I could think of to alienate myself from the neo-conservatives who believed their power was unshakable.

I put slogans like "On the Wednesday meeting, she'll be tripping" on my campaign flyers. One night, while working on my political campaign and being kind of high and manic from the energy of pure irreverence, a friend of mine said "Bok Choy, I think you just need to run on a platform of 'Free Crack.'" I loved it. We eventually modified it to "Free Crack! And Everyone Get's Laid!" in an attempt to be more inclusive. Still, I thought it brilliant.

My, how that one really got to the recovering drug addicts (yes, there were a handful of Narcotics Anonymous attendees at Twin Oaks) and persuaded them to join in the pool of people who were simply exasperated from being pissed at me.

The truth was, there came a point where I held nothing sacred. To the people of Twin Oaks, especially the lifers, this social experiment was their life and they held it dearly and treated it with reverence. For me, I was like a rebellious teenager with nowhere to go. I was broke in every sense of the word. And I hated it. All of it. I hated that I didn't have shoes and that the gravel on our walking path was sharp and jagged. I hated that strawberries were rationed and bras were outlawed. I hated the way the young college girls on the farm for the visitor programs sparkled and shined, not yet aware of what they would lose after it was too late to go back. I hated my stupid boyfriend, who controlled my time and emotional energy and demanded that we "process" our feelings for hours each night. I was all pissed off with nowhere to go. Or so you could say.

Learning to Fire Hoop

The big shift seemed to happen all at once, during my first spring. It started with the mohawk. In an instant, when I got my hawk, a veil shattered like glass and I was suddenly set free from a beauty standard I wasn't even aware was oppressing me, but once liberated I vowed I would never go back to. This unnamed oppressor was the the pressure to be pretty. When I saw my head in the mirror, I saw myself in a completely new light. I wasn't pretty anymore. It was a simple and plain reality. But there was no failure in this realization, which was surprising to me. I was something else entirely. And it bordered on dangerous.

It was aslo during this time that I learned to fire hoop. Fire hooping is a bit of a less commonly known fire performance art than, say poi or fire juggling. It demands full body engagement to direct the hoop, and simply the power required to fuel the movements demanded an expression of raw energy that felt at times more powerful than sex.

During my initiation to the art, I was left with dark blue and purple bruises all over my body- from wrist to hip to ankle- anywhere the hoop made contact with my flesh due to its massive weight. Fire hoops are heavy. And big. I would hoop for hours, until I could bear no more, and then itch to return to it while my body developed greater and greater resistance and endurance to a conditioning which bordered on abuse.

Hooping is a true art and for many a spiritual practice. You need the hoop to make contact with you in order for the dance. It pushes against you, and you push back. It reacts, and continues moving. You wait again for contact. Over time, you negotiate with it. You push back harder. And faster. You tease it from the security of your hips to new places. Always promising a time to linger and experience the new rhythm once it arrives at its assigned destination.

But then the moment comes when your hoop completely yields its destiny to you. And your body. And you bring the art to unimaginable climaxes. With fire spinning in rings ten feet over your head, only to come back forcefully with an arm that can throw it back in the air in a moment's notice. Or to be grabbed by your shoulder and fiercely throw and choke you as fire lights up a face that stopped being afraid of the heat long ago. A neck that craves the heat and a flesh that feels a tangible satisfaction when metal from the wick makes that satisfying sound of hair and skin being singed. Holding a record on the body itself.

A Mohawked Anarchist Punk Chick

So here we have the ingredients for my ensuing insanity. A disillusioned Choy, pissed at her home, freshly mohawked, who has found a way to hack to the labor system making and selling wine and fire hooping. At times I hooped 6 hours a day for practice. I didn't really understand it at the time, but the movements from the hooping was helping to keep me safe on an energetic level.

I got swept up in Circus culture. As a way to make actual money, I rode into Charllotesville, Virginia each Friday night with some of my friends and we busked and performed for money. We rarely left with more than $30 each for our efforts. Enough to buy a goat's herder cheese and cracker spread at the Twisted Branch cafe, an popular hang out space for us punks and street performers. That or a bag of magic mushrooms.

My life seemed to begin to revolve around producing and consuming drugs and alcohol and fire performing. I learned which of these hobbies overlapped and which did not pretty quickly. For example, drinking and hooping was a big no-no. I discovered that while laying on the courtyard face up, watching the sky spin to a spilled jar of sour cherry saki, freshly brewed by yours truly.

But MDMA and hooping was a wild success! Pain turns to pleasure on this drug, and your connectedness to the rhythms pushing the hoop and pulsating through your body push you to the edge of what's possible. I could find myself teasing my hoop up my body to my face, which generally is too delicate to hoop on, to a move where I would transition the hoop from my forehead to my shoulder no handed. The music would affect the performance as well, whether it was a drum circle or simply the Talking Heads blasting from my stereo. Hooping to Sand in the Vaseline never got old.

Something really weird happened to me by the time my first summer came around at Twin Oaks. I stopped believing I could live anywhere else. I both hated Twin Oaks and felt I needed the community to survive. I started being afraid of "the mainstream." It was a really weird dynamic. Because even when things became total hell for me and I planned to leave, I still planned to come back. The truth was, nine months in, I had become totally brainwashed.

I actually took a vacation in July and rode my bicycle 500 miles across Iowa with my family on a bike ride called "RAGBRAI". I brought my fire hoop and busked at night. The money was pretty great, about $75 for every 15 minute set I performed. Because money was so hard to come by at the commune, I saw this as a huge opportunity to get ahead financially. So I worked hard, performing multiple sets a night strategically in high traffic areas filled with a lot of drunk guys, which is always where the money is for fire hooping.

A fire-performing juggling troupe caught wind of what I was doing, perhaps acknowledging that we were competing for the same audience, and invited me to perform with them. They made promises they couldn't keep, like that I would make more money with them than as a solo performer, but I was excited to meet new people and join another circus community, so I agreed to perform with them for the rest of the ride. What I didn't know was that this troupe would become like an extended family to me during my twenties and set the scene for my epic bicycle ride three years later.

When I came back from my vacation "off the farm," I gained the strength to exit my relationship with my boyfriend, the man with the white gloves. The strength came mostly from a 19 year old girl who saw something in me I had forgotten. I met with him and informed him in the simplest terms I knew how what our new arrangement would be moving forward: that he would never touch me again and never come into my room again.

I went to my room, locked the door, and climbed up into my loft for bed. The walking compost receptacle, as was his nickname, pounded on the door until the small lock yielded, climbed up the loft, cornered me, and began an assault, both verbal and physical. While squeezing my ribs with such force my psyche chose to leave my body and become an observer, he screamed "You're nothing without me! Don't you know what I do for you? Don't you know what people say about you? You need me!"

All I could get out was, "Stop it, you're hurting me." He squeezed harder. Demanded further. "Stop it, you're hurting me." I don't remember all the details. Just that eventually he left. In the morning I looked at my naked abdomen in the mirror. Deep blue and black marks had made their impression all along my rib cage. Years later, a girlfriend would ask me "Jenell! Why didn't you call the police?"

You may have asked yourself a similar question. I will simply respond with the truth that we were all really brainwashed at this place, especially toward "the establishment," which included the police. "Radical Anarachists" we liked to think, or deluded ourselves to be. Even our five-year-olds were involved in the brainwashing. Adults would play with them while chanting: "The Police! Are Not! A Neutral Institution! They Maintain The Status-Quo of the Ruling Elite!" to which the children would chime in, singing and chanting over and over with more force and passion with each repetition.

The truth is for me, the police have never protected me. First, as a mohawked punk who did a lot of drugs, then as someone with a mental health diagnosis that wasn't properly treated or under control for a long time. The way the police interacted with me historically has been lacking at best and unethical at worst. I have found myself naked and cold on a cement floor, denied a blanket because I hadn't "earned it" because clearly I was suicidal, pushed around and called "stupid" because I thought I had the right to remain silent when under arrest.

But this story isn't about the police or my distrust and disdain for their treatment toward me. This is a story about my bike ride. Bok Choy's bike ride. My relationship with the police will end up fueling my bike ride, as I will be wrongfully arrested and taken into custody at the request of my father, who's privilege as a white anglo-saxon protestant male would, time and again, afford him the upper hand in our interactions when we were in conflict. The result of this arrest would leave me homeless and so broken that any risk could only improve my lot.

But so it is that there was always grace amid the confusion and pain. Now, looking back, I can see clearly that there was always love. At the time, I couldn't always see it or feel it. In the end, I would rediscover a flame within that I could trust with my whole heart. A true love would find me and speak to me in a way I could understand. In matras around a ten dollar bicycle. In the way a stranger would give me $8 dollars and a fresh slice of blackberry pie. I learned to trust in a supernatural provision from an abundant source that wants to provide richly for all of us. How coming close to death in the mountains of Pennsylvania would bring me closest to love and true community in a way I could never orchestrate or produce from my imagination. I am so humbled and excited to share this story with you. So let me bring you to So let me bring you up to speed and catch you up.

Part 2

After Twin Oaks, Before the Bike Ride

Budapest

I stayed at Twin Oaks for approximately 2 years. After my second summer, I went straight away to a very prestigious study abroad program for mathematics in Budapest, Hungary. I had dreamt of this opportunity for years now, and the fact that I was unable to attend years ago was a big factor in my decision to drop out of college before senior year. Looking back, I think I was a spoiled and entitled brat. If I wasn't going to have my education the way I wanted, I simply wasn't going to have it all. But my time at the commune changed my financial aid situation. And so, soon after living a very bizarre and brainwashed experience on a farm full of facism, drugs, rape and hospitals, I found myself, still mowhaked, in a very confusing world.

I did not adapt to living abroad as well as I thought I would. I was older than my classmates by two or three years. And I had a really hard time relating to them. They were pampered, sheltered rich kids from name brand schools who hadn't seen the shit of the world. The girls looked like porcelin dolls to me. And Hungary was facing a lot of economic and social challenges when I arrived. I couldn't focus on the math for a variety of reasons. I was not the same girl who had held this dream in her heart three years ago.

I slipped into a horrible depression and left the program after only 7 weeks abroad. I flew back to Iowa and stayed in my childhood home which my father had gotten in the divorce. I slept on a shitty air mattress and went about two months eating almost nothing and getting up only to pee. I recall my younger sister coming home for a visit and expressing how upset she was because I was thinner than she was. No one took me for any real help for my depression.

In the new year, I moved in with my younger sister and her boyfriend for reasons I don't quite remember. I signed up for classes at the college and my sister made me peanut butter smoothies every morning to help me gain weight. It was a very strange time. I had nothing. A twin size mattress in a nook in the attic and few pairs of clothes. I took a logic course and my first art class.

I had manic episodes which were weird and frightened my younger sister. I would bike to Wal-Mart in the middle of the night and steal bizarre items, then call the manager and taunt him with threats. I would flirt and hook up with the night stockers in the back of the parkinglot and race home on my bicycle at all hours of the night, manic as fuck and completely unaware how out of control I was.

Before the semester ended I found myself inpatient at the University of Iowa Hospitals and Clinics. During my first hospitalization, they treated me kindly. Sort of. A social worker helped me drop out of school, and all the grant money I received for the semester got refunded back to me in my checking account. At first I was so confused by this. But it was nice to have the money and I thought about the implications of this. Once again, I had found a logical loophole in the system. Naturally, I had to see how far I could take it. So I made it a point to always be enrolled in school. I learned how to hustle, this time the Federal Government. Over the 10 years it took me to complete my senior year (yes, I spent 10 years enrolled and then dropped out before completing my B.A. in Mathematics in 2015), I hustled $22,000 in cash from refunded Pell Grants.

Hospitals

The University of Iowa Hospitals and Clinics first treated my manic episode with long-lasting Haldol injections. I became mentally retarded, tired, and slow. It was very confusing to be under the influence of this medicine, feel entirely unlike myself, but get feedback from all the staff that I was "doing so well!" I was eventually released on a court committal, which required me to get an injection every three weeks and attend an outpatient day hab program. I would just sit brain-dead and tired, fantasizing about when I could lie down between classes.

For the time I spent in Iowa City with my little sister, I mostly remember just being in school, getting hospitalized for manic episodes, and then dropping out. There just seemed to be no end. I wasn't getting better, and I was very confused about my illness. I was paranoid that the doctors wanted to take something away from me that was a gift. I recall being taken to court where a doctor testified that I had said I didn't want to take my medicine because "it was stealing my manic light."

Time and again, I was told that I didn't have insight into my illness. Eventually, I found myself left with nowhere to live. I wasn't working, I was broke, and I was unstable. So, at age 24, I moved back to what felt like a no-nothing small town * in the middle of nowhere Iowa with my dad.

- Note to reader: I would like to honor the small town I called home and call home to this day. It is certainly filled with charm, safety, and wonderful people- all of whom have supported both my recovery and the writing of this book.

Part 3
Pre-Bike Ride Preparations

Meet My Dad

My dad was not well when I moved back in with him. My older sister was living at home with him and raising her young son, JD. And she took care of my dad the best she knew how. His illness manifested in subtle ways. For example, he hoarded stacks of newspapers in his office. My sister would sneak piles and piles of papers out periodically to make room in his office to sit. I saw that he was not well since the divorce and that he had his own brand of crazy going on.

Now that I had a psychiatric diagnosis of Bipolar 1, I began to lose the privilege of experiencing the full range of normal human emotions. In particular, I was not allowed to be angry. If I was angry, it must mean that I was manic. It's important to note that I buried a lot of anger toward my father before moving in with him. His illegal management of money prevented me from going to Budapest before I dropped out of college. Once I found myself at the commune, he was the one who emptied my bank account without warning or permission. When I told him what had happened because I couldn't buy a train ticket, he blamed me. He said "If you had told me what was going on, I would have bought you a train ticket-everything that happened to you was a result of your choices."

I don't remember all the details of the incident, but my father and I were arguing and he accused me of being manic. I was so sick of my emotions being undermined, that in response, I knocked over his six-foot stack of old newspapers he kept hoarded in his office. I meant this very intentionally to make a point. The point being, of course, that maybe I wasn't the only one who was crazy.

The result was that he called the local police, told them that his "Bipolar daughter" was manic, out of control, and trashing his office. But I was not manic. I was simply angry. I was taken to the hospital, but after my 48-hour hold, the doctor and judge determined they could not keep any longer because I was rational and calm. However, I decided upon release that I would never live with my dad again.

I had nothing but the clothes on my back and a public transit voucher the social worker from the hospital gave me. I took a cab to the homeless shelter in Des Moines, IA. Boy, was I out of place. I seriously almost got shanked with a broken toothbrush for playing dominoes incorrectly. Everyone wants you to buy them cigarettes and all the guys hit on you. The girls are crazy hard. I had no idea what I was getting myself into. In the day, I walked around town and then at night I ate as much food as possible and got to bed early because we had to be out by 6:30am.

Homeless on a Friend's Couch

At some point during my stay I called a friend of mine from high school and told him where I was. He asked if he could visit me during the day and offered to let me stay on his couch indefinitely. It was weird, because he didn't have his own place. He lived with his mom in a small, tiny town about 7 miles from my dad's house. But I decided to accept his invitation. For about 3 weeks, I loafed around on my friend's couch and didn't do much of anything.

I was in the lowest low of my life. Homeless. Broke. No job. No life. Going nowhere. My disconnect with my family was also painful. I had been invited to my cousin's wedding which was four months out, on the calendar for the middle of September and had been planning to make the drive to North Carolina with my dad, his girlfriend, and my older sister. But after my most recent falling out with my father he made it abundantly clear that he would have no part in taking me to the wedding any longer and that I would have to make other arrangements.

I can't really explain this in any other way than that I simply resolved that I would find a way to make it to my cousin's wedding. I just needed to make it. So I planted the seed in my subconscious. And, as ever obedient and faithful, the universe began working on finding the solution on my behalf.

The solution revealed itself to me in the most unlikely of places a few weeks later. At a garage sale. And now our story is about to begin.

Meeting My Nishiki

It wasn't so much a garage sale as this really cool estate sale on a farm where I met her. As I may have hinted at before, I had done a lot of biking in my life and I have an eye for special bikes. As my friend and I were leaving the farm where the sale took place, I noticed three vintage bicycles in immaculate condition leaning against the barn. I stopped my friend and told him I wanted to look at them before we left. And that is when I saw her:

A beautiful, 1972 blue Nishiki Century road bike. In perfect condition. And a perfect fit for my size and frame. The price: $10. I couldn't believe my luck. In an instant, like lightning hitting my brain in a divine moment of inspiration, I saw with perfect clarity the solution to my problem around finding a way to my cousin's wedding in North Carolina.

Somehow, I was going to buy that bike, and I was going to ride it across half the country to the wedding. Yes! After speaking with the owner, I learned that beautiful Nishiki was in such great condition because she had spent most of her life indoors in the barn. I literally did not have a single dollar to my name. So I did what any scrappy petty criminal would have done in such a pivotal and desperate situation: I wrote a bad check for $10. And like that, she was mine.

Training

I began my training right away. I began by bicycling the seven miles from my friend's house to my dad's house. I would sneak inside, lock myself in the bathroom, and take a long, hot bath until my father, enraged that I was in his house without his permission, would resort to cutting the power and hot water to the bathroom. It was good motivation to have to make the seven hilly miles knowing that I would have the opportunity to piss him off.

My older sister and I were still very close, and so I would also visit with her on the outside patio. Soon I could make longer distances. I began extending my daily ride to a 15 mile round-trip to the nearest "big town" (big town for Iowa). I needed some basic supplies. I took the back-rack and panniers that my dad had on his bike and put them on my own. I found a milk crate and attached it to the top of the backrack. I'm not quite sure where I got the money, but I did purchase a sleeping bag, rainjacket, and small tent from K-Mart, back when K-Mart still existed.

I was still pursuing my poetry quite seriously. I had discovered a venue when I was at the homeless shelter in Des Moines called the "Des Moines Social Club" and they had open mike poetry on Thursday nights.

Now that I had a tent and sleeping bag, I began making a week long loop that revolved around making the 50 mile trip to the Des Moines Social Club every Thursday. It looked something like this: bike from my friend's house to my dad's, visit with my sister, bike 8 more miles to a park and camp. Then the next day bike 25 miles to a college town and enjoy the trails, camp in the woods, then make another 30 miles South to a town outside of Des Moines, then finally make it to the Des Moins Social Club on Thursday, and then head back to my friend's house.

Meeting Dave

Now that I was getting serious about my training, I was getting fitter and more and more confident in my ability to make the trip successfully. I was confident because I was utterly naive about what I would be up against. Broken spokes, tornadoes, hunger, thirst, rainstorms, hypothermia, pneumonia, I had no concept of any of these possibilities which would end up as part of my manifest reality. All I knew was that, right now, in the training phase, I was having the time of my life. Especially in the college town, which had a really cool bike shop with a cat. And also all my fun at the Des Moines Social Club.

I had it all planned out. I would train this loop until RAGBRAI, which was always the last full week in July. Then I would ride across Iowa with my fire-performing team, making as much cash for my trip by performing as many sets as possible in the towns each night, and then head on East for

Boone, North Carolina. The trip, including my training, should take about four months. It felt good to have a very concrete, objective goal. But I didn't know what I would do afterward. I considered train hopping. Why stop at four months? Why not have a full year of adventures? Because train hopping is so dangerous, I thought it might be nice to see if there was anyone out there who wanted to join me.

So I did what anyone would have done at the time- I placed an ad on Craigslist describing my "Year of Adventures." I didn't have a computer, but I frequented the library in whatever town I found myself in almost every day to work on my poetry. Two people responded. One was an older man who was part of a RAGBRAI training ride and invited to train with him, with the offer of free beer. This was wonderful.

Another person answered my ad as well. His writing style was succinct and sweet. I don't remember everything he wrote, but I distinctly recall one line read "You might be the coolest girl I've never met." I was kind of flattered, and we messaged back and forth and decided to meet up at the Des Moines Social Club on open mike night. I think it might have been the Fourth of July. I think that because after we met up, we got sushi and then walked along the Des Moines River and fireworks went off and reflected off the water.

My new friend Dave was unlike anyone I had ever met. As I got to know him, I found the way he lived to be fascinating. For example, he was literally one class away from his bachelor's degree. He decided not to finish, and he was fine with that. He liked Friends more than Seinfeld. I couldn't believe I was becoming friends with someone who had every episode of Friends on DVD. When I came over to his apartment, I learned that his system for dishes was to keep every dish in his kitchen dirty and then wash each one individually on demand as needed.

One day we played "Kill, Fuck, Marry" with Rachel, Monica, and Phoebe from Friends. Dave's answer: "Kill Monica, Fuck Rachel, Marry Phoebe" Ha ha. The few weeks we hung out while I was training was a lot of fun. Dave supported the bike ride from a distance by following and commenting on my blog posts I updated along the way. It felt nice to have someone rooting for me.

Part 4
The Bike Ride

Getting Ready for RAGBRAI- excerpts from my blog

Things to do before leaving on my trip in 4 days:

- Secure housing between Chicago and DC
- Get lots of drugs from my doctor
- Make a painting and mail it
- Make a video and post it on youtube
- Mail a book to a boy
- Learn more songs to play on my trumpet

Things I should do but will not:

- Purchase cold-weather gear
- Come up with more money for the trip

Things I'm packing that I shouldn't:

- A trumpet
- A huge bag of cosmetics
- 5 skimpy little slip dresses
- Black lingerie
- Poetry Books

Things that I'm packing that I need:

- A tent
- A sleeping bag
- A camping air mattress
- Tools
- Camping Gear

- Zip-Lock Baggies
- Drugs

Things I'm debating about packing:

- A rainbow xylophone
- A huge jazz fake book

Things that I wish I was packing but am not:

- The Dream Machine (aka my sweet button accordion)
- A fire hula-hoop (I am very sore about this one...)

Things I resent packing:

- A cell phone

Comment: Dave I'm going to miss the occasional adventures. It's been a great 2 weeks. Here's hoping the draw of the east coast doesn't grab you and hold on forever

Still Packing…

Down to

- 3 dresses
- One full-length sweater
- One Blue Tiger tank-top

But I haven't decided yet:

- One pair of mushroom underwear or two?

My older sister and I are in disagreement over this one.

Comment: Dave: Go Commando! Be free

Things I will not miss for the next two months:

- My dad's verbal abuse

Things I will miss:

- Sleeping with JD and putting my hands on his warm tummy.
- Making JD oatmeal in the morning.

- Playing Pirates and Mermaids with JD.
- Being a girl with my sister.

Goals for Day 1 on the bus:

- Make a friend.
- Meet a cute boy.

RAGBRAI

Day 1: Poor-BRAI

Meet James

When I first saw James, I was intrigued and somewhat delighted. The way he drove our team's bus was so funny- he was bouncing up and down on the driver's seat and it seemed at times that he could barely keep his foot on the pedal. He was cute. And I'd had a few beers. I had overheard that he was a mathematician like myself, and I needed to know more. So I walked up to the driver's seat, sat down, and asked him the most pressing question on my mind:

"James, are you Zorn's Lemma or the Axiom of Choice?" He immediately took his eyes off the road, and with a twinkle and an amused smile, responded

"The Axiom of Choice."

I loved his answer. Because that meant I could be Zorn. This would be a fun game to play. So I decided to experiment with pulling his attention toward me in a ridiculous way, in a potentially dangerous way. In Zorn fashion, I decided to kiss him. James responded to the invitation, kissed me back and kept driving. This went on for over an hour while our entire team watched, in a bit of shock, amusement, and speculation.

As strapped for cash as I was, everyday was a hussle. Especially getting food. My budget was $1 per day, until further notice, depending on how well I made out with fire hooping money on the ride. It seems impossible, but I just met it as one of many challenges to overcome to make it to my cousin's wedding on time. For example, on our way to the Missouri River, our bus stopped at Mexcian place where a burrito is $7. I noticed that a side of rice and beans was $1 and asked the manager if he would make me a rice and bean burrito and sell it to me for $1. He ended up giving me a free burrito plus a grapefruit soda. This is the kind of thing that eventually became the norm rather than the exception for me. Sometimes people would question and ask why and how I always seemed to end up with nice and free stuff- things like a whole box of shot-blocks and expensive food. Eventually, the answer simply became "because she's Bok Choy."

Because of my somewhat reckless and public display of affection toward James, by the time we arrived at the Nebraska/Iowa border for the beginning of the ride, our team assumed that we must be together. Now that I was really beginning my adventure, I was embracing my liberty and felt anything was possible. James was a bit of an intrigue, but I never planned to sleep with him or pursue anything beyond an innocent flirtation.

He was planning his own solo bike ride after RAGBRAI. We had a lot of common interests but he wasn't exactly my type in a lot of ways. He had the body of a body builder and he was a bit short. I like broad and tall with softer edges. His hair was buzzed as well, and I've always been weak for a good head of hair. But what it really came down to was that he rode an aluminum frame bicycle with a carbon fiber fork. I was tinsel steel and steel with pride. And ultimately this was the fundamental reason why James and I were incompatible. Because his bike was a yuppie bike.

* Note to Reader: *The reason why I can't stomach an aluminum frame with a carbon fiber fork isn't just that it's a yuppie bike. There is status in being able to bike fast, so the lighter the better. Aluminum is light and cheap, but nearly impossible to handle because it's so stiff. Carbon fiber, on the other hand, is both light but has a flex. The yuppie who buys an aluminum frame with a carbon fiber fork wants all the status and control without throwing down the cash for a full-on carbon fiber bike.*

Natc Manly

As soon as we set up for camp my eyes locked on the hottest. guy. ever. He was wearing a utili-kilt and he walked with a spring of joy in his step. He was tall, covered in tattoos, and super sexy. I smiled at him and he looked at me, and then said to the guy with him, loud enough for me to hear "I like her hair!"

Later, after our team put on our first fire show of the ride, I saw him again near camp. I walked up to him and said "Are you that boy I like?" I have no idea what possessed me to ask such a weird question. I never claimed to be all that smooth with boys. But it was late and I asked for help setting up my tent. Then we made out and had raw and hot tent sex. And It never really occurred to me that my entire team could hear everything. And they were not happy about it.

People often mistake me for having a higher level of awareness than I actually have. Because I'm good at math, people think I'm smarter than I am. It didn't occur to me that hooking up with Nate Manly (yes, isn't his name even sexy?) would bother James in the least or the people who were loyal to him. I mean, all we did was make out for an hour on the bus. So what?

Day 2: Hungry-BRAI

Today I also spent a total of $1 on food. My bike was sucking and I was hungry and cranky all 77 miles.

Day 3: James-BRAI

Today I biked with James. He fixed my bike which ruled and then decided to push me up all the hills, which also ruled. In the heat of the day, we came across a giant slip and slide down a huge hill into a pool. With out a moment's hesitation, James stripped down naked, doused himself with dish soap water, and slid down head first. Everyone was cheering. And holy fuck. He has an amazing body. Even if he is a little short.

Later in the day, we found a party station where girls could get free temporary tattoos on the condition that they were applied with beer and then men licking the beer over the tattoos to adhere them. I had my camera, and James pretended to do a news coverage on this event while I recorded him on video. He interviewed one woman who was getting a tattoo on her upper inner thigh.

James was pretty valuable to the team, with both his presence and resources. He owned the bus and was paying for all the gas. But he also occupied a space for problem solving, strength, responsibility, and resolve. What I liked about him was that he liked to play. And that he was smart.

We both loved math and bikes, so we could have ridiculous conversations that I couldn't so easily find with other people- like taking the concept of a Brunnian Ring and translating it into a bicycle. We joked about our imaginary "Brunnian Bike" that would completely disassemble and fall apart if even one piece found its way out of place.

I tried to draw pictures of the Fano Plane for James on napkins at a diner we found ourselves eating at in the late of the night. Even in my failure to capture the perfection of three connected with itself in such perfect symmetry that is pushes itself into the third, then fourth dimension, James seemed to intuitively understand that sometimes what we see is so beautiful that it cannot be perfectly captured. Not on a dingy napkin, at least.

Despite our similar interests and attraction, in my world, I certainly was not planning on falling in love with James. James was a bit of an intrigue, but nothing more. Besides, the past few years had left me so bruised and broken, love was simply a luxury that I did not have. I was clawing and fighting my way for a freedom from something I could not name. But it was real and tangible. It was a never ending dirty grit on my brow. Mixed with sweat and dripping into my eyes, causing a stinging blur that needed to be flushed out. And I needed every ounce of strength to fight it. I certainly couldn't give myself away to anyone. Not now.

Day 4: Nate Manly-BRAI

The night before riding with Nate Manly, I found myself sleeping in James' tent and we ended up fooling around a bit, but nothing really happened. Like I said, I never intended things to go too far. The next day, when Nate met up with me for our ride together that day, he asked me if I slept with James because had noticed how flirtatious he was being around me at camp. I told him no, that we just fooled around for a little bit. Nate just laughed and called me a slut in a way that didn't offend me, because I was in denial about my behaviors.

Nate was pure fun, sex, and play. He was really exciting to be around. The sex was really good, but the playing was even more fun. Like today- Nate dressed up as Superman and everytime he pushed me up a hill he posed like he was flying.

I met a guy with a pocket trumpet and we played together in front of a crowd for the RAGBRAI documentary and it was awesome. However, I was a little bit nervous playing on camera so I asked the audience if anyone had sunglasses I could borrow to help me feel more at ease. Nate eagerly offered up his. He told me his were special because there was a lightning bolt Hello Kitty sticker on the side, and that it gave the glasses super powers.

I spent my $1 on a pickle today.

Day 5: I Don't Remember This Day-BRAI

I don't remember a ton about today except that by the end, just before riding into camp, I stopped and had 7 beers. I have no idea why I did this. But at the time, drinking definitely helped me feel better about sex. Nate was planning on stopping by and I definitely wanted to hook up before he headed back to his own "tent city" as he called it. To my surprise, James was waiting for me at the entrance of my tent. Like he just totally couldn't take a clue. I just sat inside my tent, drunk and frustrated, while Nate and James chatted civilly. Why on earth was James cock-blocking me? What was wrong with him?

Eventually, after Nate and I hooked up again and were eating food on the bus, he said to me

"You're not very observant, are you?"

"What?"

I had no idea what he was talking about. Then he pointed to the wedding ring on his left hand. Holy crap. It had never occurred to me to look for a ring. What the fuck was wrong with this guy? He's on vacation and cheating on his wife? And then he's making a casual comment almost blaming me for not knowing?

We talked, and the story got even worse. His wife just had their first baby two weeks ago. She was home alone, with a newborn, and her husband is on vacation fucking around. And I was complicit in this. Fuck this shit. I was so pissed. So pissed off at what I had participated in. Pissed off that I was such a poor judge of character, or that maybe this simply was the character of the opposite sex. I was pissed that I was entirely heterosexual, and that I had to deal with this half of the population in such a personal and intimate way.

But then instead of just civilly ending it and parting ways, I had sex with him one more time. I smacked and pushed him around in a way that communicated my disdain as I tried to take something from him that I felt he didn't deserve anymore.

* Note to Reader: *As I thought about it, I realized Nate's bicycle was one of deceit. To the world, he rode a beautiful American made bicycle with braze-ons he applied himself. A Cannondale. But that wasn't the bicycle that I knew him to be. To me, Nate was a neon retrofitted fixed gear bike that was the envy of all the hipsters in the Twin Cities. He was always showing off his fun and playful nature. But he couldn't sit still. Even when the light was red he did trackstands. Fucking around but going nowhere.*

Day 6: “Roll Your Own-BRAI”

Today I rode with James again and had fun. I met a Suzzi from the Iowa Marching Band! We stopped in towns and played Iowa Hawkeye tunes and I finally learned all the alternative lyrics to "Roll Along"

“Roll You Own, Roll Your Own, Iowa Home Grown! On to getting stoned…”

The Medicine man tended to my wounds today again. He wrapped my ankle. I liked it. It stormed in town so we did our show for the camp. I liked that too. We watched it on top of the bus. Our team captain is such an amazing performer. He juggled fire while on a tall unicycle, among other things.

Day 7 "Bok Choy is out of Salt-Brai"

Today I felt like shit. I had a headache behind my eyes and my tummy hurt way bad. So I stopped at the coffee place and sipped peppermint tea for about two hours. But I never felt better. I just wanted to puke and my eyes hurt. So I went to the Medicine man and he told me I needed salt and the prescription to my illness was three pickles and a cup of pickle juice. He did not charge me. I liked that. A pickle was my medicine. I found a helmet on the side of the road.

I stopped at a trucker weigh station and had my bike weighed. 80 lbs. By the time our entire team made it to the Mississippi River, on the Iowa/Illinois border, Nate and his team were long gone. We rode into Burlington, Iowa and the river was wonderful. We all swam in it and had fun. I built a super cool raft and floated down it for a while.

Nate had stopped by camp and left me a bunch of supplies for my tour and wrote me a long letter. The support crew all seemed moved by this gesture and kept telling me how much they thought that he was just the nicest guy.

My affair with Nate catapulted me into the sluttiest week of my life- where in the course of 7 days I would sleep with 4 different guys. First with Nate, then a random guy from New York named Tony who was on his own tour, then with a guy I knew in Chicago, and finally, after over a week of nothing but 100% hard core pursuing and calculated attention where I was the most starved- that being around my writings, I would give in to James' advances. And this would change the trajectory of my entire adventure.

Day 8 “Sunrise Over the Mississippi”

Today I woke to the sun rising over the Mississippi. The lure of the river is overwhelming and makes the whole town feel good. I am glad to have the day off. I am glad that I'm touring alone. I am glad my cell phone is gone. I'm glad that I might leave Iowa and never come back.

Things I may or may not do today:

- Tend to my wounds properly
- Swim
- Play on the Bridge
- Read
- Play my Trumpet
- Eat Food

Day 9: Crossing the Mississippi Burlington, IA-Victoria, IL

Last night I screamed like crazy in my tent because I woke up and it was so small. The cool thing about touring after RAGBRAI is all the cycling tourists hang out together. I met a boy named Tony who gave me an orange whistle and some good advice. He is the boy who gave me his wisdom about gumption. About how I may not have all the gear, knowhow, or money, but I made up for that with gumption. We also hooked up under a bunch of pine trees outside the laundry mat-making steady progress toward my sluttiest week of all time.

*Note to reader: *I make no comment about Tony's bicycle because it was as memorable as his lovemaking. Nothing noteworthy.*

My bike looks f*ing adorable with its new tiny stuff on the back. I ate a lot of food yesterday and for breakfast, which ruled. I had fries, chicken, fruit, corn, spicy V8, and a parfait with little gummy worms on top. I ate a whole bag of Rannier cherries. I think I'm going to do this like once a week- rest and eat. I'm crossing the Mississippi today, heading out on 34 (SCARY) for 8 miles, and then going up on 164. My goal today is to acquire a map of Illinois.

I miss my sister. I wish I had a cool dog. I wish my body was stronger. When I biked into Victoria, IL, I was ready for bed. I saw a house with mushrooms and gnomes on the porch, and decided to ring the bell. Long story short, I got my own house, my own yard, and a cold shower. I was pleased. It rained in the night. I woke up to my entire body itching. I scratched for about half an hour and then coated my skin with first-aid lotion. On the road, my inner tube popped and I saw a dead turtle.

Day 10: Victoria, IL- Princeton, IL

I need a bike shop! I need a bike shop! My back tire is out of true and it's rubbing against the rear brake with every rotation. It seems the closest one is about 50 miles away. I wonder if I'll make it. I wonder if my exposed skin can take any more direct sunlight in the heat of a midwest summer. Or if the Semis whizzing past me will miss me when there is literally no shoulder to ride into. After pulling over several times to make adjustments I have no experience or know how to make, I just begin to repeat to myself:

"All that I have is all that I need. All that I need is all that I have"

As silly as it sounds with my limited means, I broke down and purchased a charger for my phone today, and then broke it the minute I tried to use it. I now have $30 left until the first, and my bicycle still needs professional help. I needed a mega adhesive remover and made friends with the body shop in town. So far, the body shops I have stopped in have all been very cool.

Day 11: Princeton-Sugar Grove

Today ruled. Even though I had a broken spoke. I met this guy named Marc with a "c" who made it very clear to me that the "c" is important- it makes him special. I couldn't have had more fun. He invited me into his home to crash on the couch and we talked for a long time and then I just woke up lying on the couch with a blanket tucked around me. Ha ha! I must have just fallen asleep midsentence! And how quietly sweet that he tucked me in.

We woke up and picked blackberries for breakfast and then we went to this little breakfast place and bakery in town. When we arrived at the bakery, a bunch of the little baking ladies excitedly presented Marc with a "c" with a pie they made from the blackberries he had brought in the other day. What was so funny was how this actually pissed him off. After we placed our orders- me with a bagel and Marc with a "c" with three chili dogs- he told me that he didn't donate the berries in order to get a pie. He just wanted it to be a gift.

We went on a car ride to Peru to the bike shop. I didn't want to hitch, but I also wanted to hang out with Marc with a "c" in the car, so I compromised my values this one time. The bike shop fixed my bike for $10, which ruled. As we parted ways, Marc with a "c" gave me all the cash he had in his walet- $8. It felt so sincere and sweet.

Today on the road I thought about politics. I biked to James' mom's house because he offered to let me stay there the night before I headed into the city. I hit a trail on the way. I saw awesome mushrooms! I was SO happy! It's mushroom season! I was hungry and couldn't find anywhere to eat and hang out except the local country club. Boy, was I out of place! I ordered fries and water and just sat at the bar while people looked and then then looked away from me.

At James' mom's house, I got a shower, maps, bike lights, laundry, and a bed- everything a wayward traveler could want. I also got a phone and talked to friends, which was nice. Tomorrow I ride into Chicago.

Roadside Advice: Meeting Your Social Needs

Touring can be lonely! Especially when you're riding alone. So how do you meet your social needs on the road? Here are my thoughts/advice.

1. Accept that touring alone is a solitary experience. Simply accept it and don't go into it lightly. Consider touring alone as "social fasting." It can be difficult, spiritual, health promoting (mentally), and make you appreciate your rooted social network much more. There is a subtle difference between loneliness and solitude, and expect to experience both. Solitude on the road can be a time of contemplative reflection by yourself, uninterrupted by all the noise. Loneliness can be just that. Lonely. Knowing that you can get comfortable and get through the loneliness will make you a stronger person.
2. I make a point to connect socially in three basic ways. First, I always get coffee in the morning. Sometimes at a mom and pop place and occasionally at a coffee shop. I make time for this and never rush it. For me, I am peppiest in the morning, as I'm both drinking coffee, excited about where I'm going, and have not yet been spoiled by the grunge of the day. I usually take this time to look at my map and do my chatting and flirting.
3. While on the road, I sometimes stop at auto body shops and sort of hang out a bit. This may sound weird, but I have found that body shops have cool people who sort of like hanging around. They're usually filled with smart people who can help you with basic mechanic questions you might want to know. Not necessarily about bikes per say, but useful knowledge nonetheless. This may just be my thing, but my advice regarding this is to learn conversational mechanics.
4. Last, chat up townies in your end town and make friends. After you've made a friend who is willing to host you, you'll have the opportunity to make a meaningful connection with another human

being one on one. This is actually a very special opportunity to exchange concentrated attention with another person. You meet very different people every time, and this interrupts the monotony of the riding wonderfully. For me, making these connections is the highlight of the day. They give me something to look forward to when 70 miles seems so far.

In summary, I expect to start and end my day with social connection while being prepared for very little during the ride. I suggest that solo-tourists make the effort to come to appreciate this time alone with yourself and make the most of it, as it is special and rare.

Archive: Dad, I'm not depressed

Dad, I don't appreciate hearing second hand from conversations with my sister that you think I'm depressed. I'm sick of you having a negative opinion about everything I do. I'm eating lots of drugs at the right times. Getting tons of Vitamin D. I have enough money to get what I need. I'm going to Chicago today and I have lots of friends there. I found a helmet on the road. You can call Uncle Stan if you want to check on me. Or you can comment on the blog. I don't know what else you're concerned about. I would prefer if you came to me with your concerns. In fact I am asking you to do that. In case I run out of salt. Or get hit by a Semi. I will say I love you. Or at least that I'm trying.

Day 12: Chicago!

Today is going to be a good day. I can tell. James' mom rules and fed me well. She had a ton of awesome books and gave me a book to keep. I got to read today on the porch. I was starved for it. I lounged around the house for several hours because it felt so good to be there. No one seemed to mind, though I should leave soon. Let it be said that I appreciate suburban comfort. I had hazelnut in my coffee and slept on nice sheets. I ate well and showered well, and played with a cute doggie. I couldn't complain about a thing if I never left a house like this again.

I am clean and my hair looks good and I put on makeup and I'm going to ride only 40 miles to get to the city, all on bike path. I'm stoked. I'm meeting new people today. Mr. Gary for one. He's one of James' friends who is offering to host me should I need a couch. I hope he's cool. I talked to my older sister on the phone last night and we both cried because we miss each other. I miss her so so so so much, and I wish I could just take her with me whereever I go.

Update: Today sucked. I still do not know how to read trail maps outside of the context of road maps, and I got screwed. I do not have a way to gauge distance when I am not using a road map. I lack a watch and a speedometer. So I figured I would just guess when I had gone 40 miles. But that did not exactly work, as it was cloudy and the riding was fine. I biked a solid 25 miles north out of my way. Then I humiliated myself by asking a cop for directions. I was thoroughly a bitch about it, but still. He was a cop. Two things really piss me off: back-tracking and cops. And today the two were combined. Sigh. But everything was Ok in the end today. I took the train and borrowed cell phones and found a boy named X that I know.

X is another mathematician who went to the same graduate school the boy I loved went to. The boy I love apparently showed X some of the books I had made him and then emailed me and told me he wanted to meet me. After graduation, X moved to Chicago to work for a hedgefund. Prior to my bike ride, he and I met at a party in Chicago and we had a really fun and playful love affair. I remember we went out for sushi and got drunk on saki and made out in public while I leaned on a lamppost under a dark sky. I thought he was down for anything. I thought he was sexy. Ethnically he was "India" Indian, and he had an exotic appeal.

What I didn't know was I had caught him at his most playful moment. Once he got oriented at work, he became obsessed with making money and had limited energy for play. He was young and learning the ropes under a lot of pressure at work to perform. Now, staying with him for the the second time six weeks later, things were different. In some ways crashing with him was excellent. He was a wealthy Indian vegetarian, so he had excellent drinks and produce on hand in his house, like mango juice and avocados. His living space was comfortable and luxurious. His apartment was in Wicker Park, so there was a lot going on. But X was exhausted whenever we would hang out, and the sex wasn't really that exciting. I think he was just tired.

Chicago Day 2

My first morning waking up in X's apartment after meeting up the night before, I woke up with all the suppressed aches and pains my body has been holding for two weeks rising to the surface. And I woke up so late that I felt scuzzy. I didn't want to move. Some parts of me couldn't. I wanted to just hang out in my bathrobe and rest and eat apples all day and write letters and other little things. I wanted to mail my older sister a poetry book I was working on putting together on the road.

But I finally got out and biked around the city. I had SO much fun. I wasn't loaded down and I was just zipping around traffic and meeting other bikers. I biked about 25 miles. I visited two cool bike shops. I found that after Semis on country roads, I have no fear of the cars in the city going 30 MPH. It felt good to feel fearless. I biked around until I found my cousin's house and hung out with her and my aunt for a while. How I found them was I just discovered by accident the avenue they live on and just followed it until it led to their house. It took a couple hours to actually arrive because they were so far north of my starting point. My aunt was so sweet- I interrupted dinner and she cut her salmon fillet in half and placed it on a plate for me. I headed back to meet up with X. Soon after I left I popped two inner tubes. I was basically just super pissed. It was late and I was tired but everything turned out Ok when this cool Albanian guy saw my misery and got me alcohol, food, and took me to X's apartment. It was like he was a magic angel or something.

Tomorrow my goals are:

1. Get my bike in order and figure out how to stop the madness of all my flat tires
2. Get to Working Bikes and volunteer if I can
3. Pay off my debts

Chicago Day 3

Today I got my bike fixed at my favorite bike shop in the whole world, thus far: Rapid Cycle on North Ave. The mechanics were super cool and smart and they let me watch and help fix without protest, as though that was the natural way in their shop. I again tried to get to Working Bikes and did not. But I did eat food that I cannot talk about. I biked downtown along the lake and met some cool young drifters, one of which held that secret zine about train hopping that only the hobos control. I hate it when they act so smug and secretive about it. I deserve it too!

The lake was cold and I knew I shouldn't swim in my clothes but I did anyway. I met a cool cyclist who also tours at the lake and he told me about Handle Bar, a cyclists bar. I had never heard of such a thing. I went to Navy Pier and had a magical evening with a magic man who liked to play as much as me, maybe more. The magic show he put on utterly delighted me and he signed my moleskin journal with a signature that may be as fantastic as my own. (In case you did not know, when I sign "Bok Choy", it forms the shape of a dancing seahorse with a mohawk) I totally get that Navy Pier is a tourist destination, but I am freaking bike touring! I also saw shiny dancers and played on a ferris wheel.

Then I went to the Handle Bar on the 2400 Block on North. It was perhaps the coolest bar I have ever been to. Actually, it absolutely was. There was bike parking in the back inside the patio and the seats were made out of bike parts. The drink specials were hilarious and the staff were having so much fun with everyone and it was just filled with super cool people and I recommend it to everyone who comes to town. My bartender was super cute and he had these really flirty tattoos: a little heart just above each of his elbows, but on the back of his arm. So even when he wasn't facing you, it felt like he was sending out vibes.

I got drunk and wrote probably the most depressing story I have ever written, and it felt good to be in the groove of free flow writing. I have been wanting to write all week. I hope I do again tomorrow. Tomorrow I get to see my cousin Hobbes and his wife for lunch. James is coming down today, too, which means I'll have a cell phone.

Chicago Day 4

Today I had lunch with my cousin and his wife. It was nice for two reasons. They are really high quality people and I ate really well. I got mini corn dogs and a pile of fries. While my cousin's wife and I were waiting outside in line, we saw this girl who looked like she went out clubbing the night before and was trying to orient herself back home after a one night stand. The entire line was watching her and laughing. When her taxi finally came and picked her up, everyone in line applauded. That was just what the vibe in Chicago was when I was there. Everyone was young, but not too young, and having a good time.

I biked around and went to an outdoorsy store and got my Keen sandals relaced for free, which ruled. Then I spent too much money on cool outdoorsy gear, which I feel mixed about. I spent the day wandering and shopping and playing at the beach. At 9p, I went to a bar and drank Monster after Monster and ate pickles until midnight. X and I met up and resolved many of our differences which was great and now we are friends again. Our argument was insanely absurd, about how he would never drink well water regardless of his circumstance. I was having issues with how delicate he seemed to be becoming. In the end, a metaphor birthed from our common tie with mathematics helped us reconcile. He may not drink well water, but we agreed that we are simply orthogonal vectors.

To the Reader: Let me just level with you about X. As we parted ways, I realize that unlike James, he is a full on carbon fiber framed bicycle that he rides to survive a race he isn't fully aware he doesn't have to participate in when it starts to suck his soul. Yes, he's also a young, urban professional. But he owns it and is honest about both his desire for wealth and status as well as his loneliness.

Tomorrow I plan to:

1. Mail stuff to my sister and
2. Buy cool stuff from Army Surplus.

Chicago Day 5

After X and I parted ways I met James at midnight. He was riding his red Ducati motorcycle. We biked, him real slow and me real fast, to Mr. Gary's house and deliriously chatted on the porch until 5am. I was up on monster drinks and they made me feel very strange. We slept in until super late. I mailed a lot of things today, and then went to Army surplus. I got a sweet sweater for the mountains and some wool socks. Things I need, but expensive nonetheless. I wanted a super cool hiking watch that could go underwater and that had a compass and such, but did not find anything like that there.

James and I played in Chicago all day, and it was my most fun day in the city. We saw lots of cool things and I met some really cool women who were interested in some of the same ridiculous literary genres as me and we swapped numbers to trade books with the plan to eventually start a book club. There was no need to tell them I am not from Chicago, as I have every intention of making this happen the next time I'm in town.

At nighttime I wanted to show James the Handle Bar, but after realizing that he doesn't drink and I didn't really want to, we went for a late night bike ride instead. We played a game where James wore all the road score we found, and when I spotted a silky thin red piece of fabric, James screamed "SASH! THAT SCREAMS SASH!" After affixing the sash on James I spotted some blue tape for extra jazz. But then after James got his sash, the game changed and he started rejecting road score that wasn't good enough for the sash. Apparently the sash could communicate with James.

The sash even rejected this super cool cape because it smelled like garbage. The ride was super fun and awesome and we saw Millenium Park and some cool sculptures and biked along the lake.

This way cute biker passed us and looked at me and smiled and said approvingly with a nod and shouted "Nice Bike!" Then he turned around and biked with us and we all talked about touring. His name was Jaimie. I was so pleased by this. I was biking at night in Chicago with a cute boy on either side of me, both super cool bike touring boys. But then we got super sleepy because it was 2:30am and we stopped to sleep by the lake. My body freaked out and I was just way itchy all over. So often, when I shed even just a little gear, I regret it. I'm getting used to having everything I need, and I wished I had my tent that night.

Chicago Day 6,7,8

Now Chicago has blurred my memory as I have been trying to leave for three days now. I keep trying to get on the train out of town, and I swear that today I will do it. I have help.

Chicago these past days has all been bikes and frisbee and boys and spicy tomato soup and sleeping in and staying up 'til five and eating Thai and having adventures and meeting awesome people and playing all day. Lots of good music, new books, another broken trumpet.

Today my goals were/are:

- Appoxy my new Hello Kitty sticker to my bike which says "This Vehicle Stops for Popcorn"
- Repack my bike
- Mail stuff home
- Get a pump and visit Jaimie at Uptown Bikes
- Get on a train and leave the city.

I am getting better and better at swapping out bad gear for good gear and at acquiring good gear in general. The people I keep meeting have been so nice and awesome when they have heard I'm touring. Thus far, I have gotten:

- An awesome tiny tent
- A whistle
- A chain, multi-tool
- Shot Blocks, carpet needle
- Knife
- Stretchy Thermal shirt
- Advice

I don't want to leave the city.

Ok: So what's up with me and James? Let me just level with you. James and I have been staying on couches at Mr. Gary's apartment, and every morning he wakes up and leaves these long beautiful comments on my poetry blog. I didn't see it coming. Looking back I can see clearly it was targeted love bombing. And I fell for it. Right on my face. Because my unrefined and immature poetry captured no one's attention. And yet it felt like my whole life. My world. Finally, after a little over a week of this, I agree to James' physical advances.

When we went into Mr. Gary's bedroom, I'll never forget the intensity of our moment of foreplay. James looked me in the dead in the eyes and said "You're in control." At first I ignored this strange comment. But he insisted on capturing my eyes and making contact. Stating again, in an absolute deliberate seriousness, he repeated: "You're in control."

What an incredibly bizarre thing to say to me right before we were about to fuck. For one, I hate making long and deliberate eye contact during sex. That fact aside, what on earth was compelling James to speak those particular words to me?

Of course I was in control. Sex was the one area of my life I would never hand control over to another person. At least not since I had been separated from the boy I loved and who still held my heart from the summer when I was 19. From another lifetime ago.

The boy who starved himself on rice and tea and was drowning in Topology in a graduate program which I felt like was taking over his whole life. His spirit. But what did I know about math anyways. And spirit in the truest sense. For me, life was still gritty and hard. And in a reality that I was in, but desperately trying to break out of, I had forgotten the joy of unbridled and unashamed love.

I had not seen this boy in two years, and his town was right in the center of the map on the way to North Carolina. I had been dead set on seeing him after I left Illinois and headed toward Indiana. To Boilermaker country. Lafayette, Indiana. Purdue University.

But once James and I started sleeping together, I suddenly wasn't so sure. I suddenly felt uneasy about seeing the boy who held my heart. The Italian mutt of a mathematician who ran on a trinary operating system consisting of math, girls, and video games. The boy who had ever gently guided me through discovering for myself the proof of the fundamental theorem of calculus over soymilk and vegan chocolate chip cookies on our first date. The boy whose mom smoked up all his child support money and never bought him a bike.

In fact, once James and I started sleeping together, I didn't want to see any other guys at all. I was planning on staying with an old boyfriend near DC for a week and that plan got sidetracked as well. While I had no way of anticipating what would take place after sleeping with James, it was like he would place a voodoo curse on me and I wouldn't sleep with another man until I met my husband, who I would meet and marry 5 years later.

A Glimpse into the Love Bombing by James

I'm including a handful of the posts James began leaving on my poetry blog between RAGBRAI and our time together in Chicago just to give you an idea of what I was up against. I am not including the actual writings because I feel that is not necessarily relevant to our story.

So here goes:

(In response to a short story about my first hospital stay)

"As I began reading this, I wondered if my imagination was sufficient for all the wonders spilled out from Bok Choy's brain. The answer is clear - a resounding no. I need my imagination to be stretched, bent, bruised and broken first. Even then I don't think I could understand, but at least it would be a start. I wish I could know these people and these places. Not only know them now in retrospect, but I wish I could also know the time that has already gone. Even though I can catch a glimpse of the truth and beauty in your words, I know there's so much more. I see you wearing your rainbow. I hear Blister in the Sun. I feel the weight of the air in 5 East when it turns away from infinite possibility to a snapshot of just one reality. I see the joy and the pain, but only through your eyes. I do not understand no matter how hard I wish. Bok Choy, you will just have to keep telling these stories over and over again until my ears bleed. Help me understand. Undoubtedly, this is one of your greatest writings."- James

(In response to a poem I wrote about a late night motorcycle ride I had with a few years back in Iowa)

“Oh, Reckless One. Does it disappoint you that each night does not end in disaster? We survived a windy night, on our cyclops (I say "our" for what was once mine becomes yours). Reading this, however, makes me think that I have failed to fail you. If tenderness is cruel, then you're in for a hard life, Reckless One.

Again and again forever on Lemmy's behalf, I apologize for such a shitty restaurant. You made an elegant feast regardless and that is just one of your talents.”

(In response to a writing about a “Self-Replicating Pattern of Love” I programmed with my old boyfriend, Jason Shark)

“This is one of the greatest things ever written by anyone. I've often wished for a world with reciprocity of feeling, but I always kill it somehow. To love as loved and to hate as hated. Such a simple little world. Elegant like a proof. You have found a piece of that world in all this chaos. Hold it tightly and invite others.”

(In response to a poem about Carbon)

“Bok Choy, this is one of my favorites. In these few sentences, you show your intelligence and passion. Distinctly, intensely - this poem is the essence of you and I love it.”

(In response to a poem exploring self-destructive desire)

“What is it that you want? Sometimes fire, sometimes ice? We all want the same ends, but the means are so complex. Burn, burn, burn. I burn this poem before it has a chance to burn me. Though my singed mind tells me it must be too late. Weakness in the aftermath doesn't count.”

(In response to a poem about inertia)

“Maybe it’s just the nerd in me, but why do I love this one so much? You need to put some of your “best of math and science” into a collection. Tell me something about your idea when you wrote this- I want to crawl into your brain. Even if I might never come out again.”

"When I read this again, I had a dream on the back of a motorcycle. There is no place we cannot go. More inertia for the moon. More still for the stars. In the end, there is no limit besides imagination. Too bad it's temporarily out of order"

And don't even get me started on this one. If this isn't manipulation and calculated love-bombing, I don't know what is.

(In response to a poem where I wrote for a dear and delightful friend and flirtation I had at the commune)

"Who, to consider you the biggest blunder, would have to be the most successful person at life ever? I've never run into anyone so perfect. Jesus could not regret. "They" say two out of three ain't bad. Surprise and Mystery are among your names. Will all you want with your lightning lips and marionette limbs- Blunderlessness."

(In response to my short-story "The Drugs in Lexington" based on my experience in locked psychiatric hospitals.)

"I told myself I would read these in chronological order this time. I give up because I'm just not ready for this one again. This story is too intense for me right now, but I want you to know that it's something I will post a better comment on later. Forgive this wuss for not being able to handle the ferocity of life as gracefully as you have. Talke to me endlessly. Tell me that everything is alright because I can only deal with reality in small doses. "I can't read" was funny in a book store on Lincoln. It's not so funny anymore. Your pain is more than I can bear-even now, so distantly related, I am how many degrees of separation from you? I can't wait to talk to you again. "

"I've accepted that reading this will never get any easier. Dark times will come and go, but the past that makes us who we are is permanent. The past is now permanent and you've got fresh scars to prove it. The good news is that you've outlived your pain. Every now and again we must dance a slow sad waltz with all the lights out, lest we forget what should not be forgotten. I Invite you to dance with me, though you can dance alone if you would prefer. Just be patient with me for not knowing how to dance- I might never know real darkness.

“ It's been a while since I've read this. It seems more familiar. Your pain was past, is present, and will be future. What calms the anger? Love. In any language.

我愛你.

wǒ ài nǐ.

Te quiero.

Je t'aime.

Ndagukunda.

Мен сені жақсы көремін.

mi do prami.

मैं तुम्हें बहुत चामता हुँ.

Ik hâld fan dy.

Ich liibe-dich.

Аз Вас обичам.

আমি তোমাকে ভালোবাস.

Iek hääb die ljoo.

Σ΄αγαπώ.
Tá grá agam duit.

Те љубам.

ഞാൻ നിന്നെ പ്രേമിക്കുന്നു.

Tshemenuadeden.

Jeu carezel tei.

ይፊትወኪ’የ!.

Ndza ku rhandza.

زه ستا سره مينه کوم.

Kei te aroha au ki a koe.

Jeg elsker deg.

Ma armastan sind.

Rakastan sinua.

ᎬᎨᏳᎢ.

كنبغيك.

Txin Yaktakuq. “

(And in response to a poem I wrote for the boy I love…)

“Isn't it beautiful the way that we can state our own axioms. "If 1=0..." When stating our axioms, we can simply say "Let 1=0..." and the rest follows easily. We prove the impossible whenever we want, whenever we need. I fear that we often need the impossible so we shape our reality to fit our axioms and continue marching along with our proofs. I understand what it's like to have an inelegant brute force proof. One missed opportunity regarding the Fano plane is weighed against the opportunities realized. You made the call because it was yours alone to make. Everyday we decide our fate among every plane in existence and theory. Fano merely forgot that the plane should have landed in London. Or maybe we still have not determined where the vertices lie. Is that why we travel?”

I hope this gives you a little backdrop into what I was up against. Why I eventually decided to sleep with James. I never seemed to be able to escape his attention. He was with me 24 hours a day in Chicago for over ten days, and even when I got on the computer to work on my poetry, there he was. Maybe, looking back, I can forgive myself for falling for him. And now let us return to our story.

Chicago Day 9: Apartment Hunting

I vowed that if I did not leave Chicago today I would begin looking for apartments.

Today I:

- Appoxied a sticker on my rear-right pannier
- Mended my torn Panniers
- Repacked my bike
- Mailed stuff home
- Went to 5 bike shops to get my back rim fixed
- Ate fries and two chocolate bars for lunch
- Was unable to find a double-walled 27" rim anywhere in the city
- Got a 700 on the back of my Nishiki for a mere $94
- Lamented that my bike no longer had all classic parts
- Set up my tent
- Ate movie theater popcorn, caramel popcorn, and dots for dinner
- Rode crazy fast on a sweet Ducati around the city
- Ate a spinach salad off of an excellent platter (*)

(*) This was in fact a reference to eating salad off James' bare abdomen while he laid on his back. Don't ask me why we did this. It was somehow in response to us going out to a horrible restaurant and so we took our salads to go and tried to "make the best of the situation" and somehow this idea came to us. It actually ended up being a really funny dinner experience for both of us and James promised to apologize every day for a year for taking me to such a shitty restaurant.

Chicago Day 10

Today I broke a Ducati Monster 620. That is all there is to say on the matter. Maybe this will finally get me out of the city. We will have to wait and see. I do not want to go to Indiana today. I want to bike up through Wisconsin and through the UP and then through Canada and down to DC. I won't get my helmet if I do this. But I don't really care anymore. I don't want to go to Indiana. Something bad is going to happen there. I can just feel it. I guess I'm not going to take the electric line then. I guess I need to look at maps again.

I gotta get out of Chicago

And all the Metra lines are NOT taking bikes due to Lollapalooza. I need to take a Metra line out of the city. We are trying to concoct a plan to get me to Kenosha, WI. Tonight. It theoretically involves a motorcycle trip to the suburbs and a long car ride to Wisconsin. Yah, I guess it's cheating. But whatever. I've gotta get out. Tonight.

Begin Wisconsin, Day 21

I spent the night on the Wisconsin border in the back of a Lexus SUV. It was full of mosquitoes and the itching was driving me to places my drugs are supposed to keep me from going. I was on a cocktail of both mood stabilizers and antipsychotics. And I was taking them. For the longest time, people always said that I was sick because I didn't take my medicine. And in part because I was receiving so much critique from my family for how I was living, I was taking my medicine almost out of spite. But I knew there was more. More to who I was and what motivated me than sickness. That sometimes I was having rational responses to insane situations. Like this one. Anyone who's entire body was itching would feel crazy. Even if he or she did not have Bipolar.

A heavy rainstorm kept me off the road until 12pm- a late start for sure, but a start nonetheless. James and I said our goodbyes on a rock by the lake until the waves crashed me to cold shrieks and I headed off on my Nishiki to an unpaved bike trail headed north along the shore. My legs got dirty.

Wisconsin has apple trees!

I met a cyclist named Paul who gave me $20 for dinner. Later, I met another cyclist named Bill who toured in his youth and biked me to the trail I was looking for. He liked my classic style, especially that I was touring in sandals. He gave me water and also $20 for "grub" as he put it. Financially, this was a sweet day. I made it into Port Washington and camped out on the beach. I left my tent and bike in search of food. I found food at a concert featuring a Beatles cover band. Yes, they had suits and wigs. I ate my fish and fries quietly while my elders drank beers and danced to songs of their youth. It made me feel weird.

Wisconsin Day 21, Port Washington-Manitowoc

I slept on the beach in Port Washington. I figured it would sound more romantic in writing than it really would be, and that I would wake up soaked by the tide, covered in sand, flashlighted by the police or to the irritation of drunk vandals. None of this happened, with the exception of a little sand. The sky was looming with flashes of light just past the horizon and I wished for a rainy Sunday. A day cold and rough enough to stay in my tent.

Today I ate like I was on a credit card tour. I had a $10 breakfast. My very favorite coffe-shop breakfast. Toasted bagel sandwich with cream cheese and veggies, coffee, and OJ. I decided to charge my phone there. I also filled up my water bottles. I heard that today was supposed to be the hottest day in Wisconsin this summer yet. I got on a trail and headed north, hoping to make it one town south of Green Bay. I saw Wisconsin corn on the way. It was dry and thin and short and fragile looking.

For the first time on my tour today I encountered the dreaded situation of not having water. I apparently filled my bottles with some sort of nasty soda instead of water. This was a problem for various reasons:

1. I was biking on a trail in the middle of nowhere
2. The soda was seriously disgusting and undrinkable
3. It was super hot and humid and I had no cloud or tree coverage

I set out to find a farmside pump and was successful. I could see little flecks of iron in the water and thought about the old days, how when a woman became anemic her midwife would prescribe a tea of boiled rusted nails. If it was good enough for them it was certainly good enough for me. Well water is my favorite vitamin water. I like pumping it. I got caught in a pretty serious storm and found shelter, along with a motorcyclist. He was super annoying, telling me things I didn't care to hear about the Airforce and the way things are.

When I finally made it back on the road, I was headed toward Manitowoc*. About 10 miles out, a woman in a van slowed beside me and hollared out the window "Are you self-contained?" Yadda yadda, her name was Kathy and I'm writing this all from her house. She has biked across the WHOLE world and across the US and Canada with Cycle America. She fed me ice cream and beer and bean soup and pomegranate juice for dinner. Next I'm headed to the late ferry for my Niskiki's first ferry ride. I've got my sailor slip-dress all ready for the ride across the lake to Michigan, where we'll begin again tomorrow, hoping to get to Canada. I wonder if Shivansh [an old math research professor] is still in Mt. Pleasant. I'm weary, washed, and fed. I hope the ferry doesn't make me throw-up.

*Manitowoc: Great Spirit

On Touring Alone

Upon hearing that I intended/am touring alone, I received a mix of reactions. Many people did not understand why someone would do this at all. Some joked that I couldn't find someone to go with me. The reactions vary somewhat but tend to fall along this vein, except when coming from a cycling tourist themselves or an experienced solo traveler. For certain, the biggest unexpected surprise I encountered during my tour was that no one tours alone. Yes, I was prepared for things like couch surfing and making friends and this and that, but what I was not prepared for was how the cycling community would receive me during this time. Or more specifically, how the touring community was looking out for me when I was not even looking, and how they were taking care of me.

Every biker dreams of touring. The benefits have at times been small and included special treatment in the bike shop, free work, and perhaps even good envy and respect. But beyond that, there is the touring network. This was the most surprising to me. This network includes cyclists who dream of touring, those who have toured in the past, and those who actively tour. This network is alive and dynamic, and the most exciting and vital part of this web is a real, live cycling tourist.

You might think you're a solo tourist. But you're not. Other tourists will spot you. And connect with you. And give you things. Well wishes and gear and money and food and showers and other special things special and practical alike. Your job in these situations is only to show appropriate gratitude. I'm a solo tourist who absolutely cashes in on the wealth of gifts available to the tourist provided by the cycling and touring communities. I think a lot of people want to be a part of something they dream of doing for the first time or again, and receiving these gifts gratefully is in fact a gift back to the the individual, while a good tour is a gift to the entire community.

On Being a Woman Touring Alone

This piece reflects my thoughts regarding the reactions I have received touring solo as a woman. From the public in general, I tend to receive dismay and confusion around how dangerous touring alone as a woman is or has the potential to be. I have a mix of verbal responses to these concerns based on the situation itself, though my thoughts remain much the same, regardless of how I play it off. I am not significantly more afraid touring solo than I am generally. My first and strongest thought around this is:

1. The world has not suddenly become a more dangerous place just because I decided to tour. The world has been a shitty place for women to live in for a long time.
2. Abuse tends to fester in stagnation, rather than motion. This is my own claim and interpretation of statical data, and I feel it is accurate. It is the woman in the abusive long-term relationship she can't get out of who is in graver danger than the woman who travels and moves and keeps her mind and body fresh with people and places. The woman in a new place is on guard and watchful. The woman who rarely leaves her comfort zone might not feel she even can at some point.
3. I'm not an idiot. I have survived my life thus far, and a little common sense keeps me pretty safe most of the time. Small things, like biking only in the day in places I don't know. Carrying useful weapons, none of which I've had to use yet. Asking around for questions I need answering. Many women have written on the topic of the "fearless woman." I love the way Margaret Mitchel did her portrayal in her novel Gone With the Wind. After Scarlett survives

> war, rape, hunger, bleeding hands and murdering soldiers, an old woman gives her a chicken and warns her that nothing is more dangerous than a woman with nothing left to fear.

The idea that woman have the option of not living in fear challenges many of the assumptions and institutions so strongly embedded in the culture of patriarchy we live in. But it is an option, and one the female population should strive to take. Seeing it all is one approach. Not being afraid to see it all is another.

Another question worth considering is what makes a woman alone more vulnerable than a woman not? If a female requires protecting, who should fill that role? It certainly cannot be fathers, boyfriends, and husbands. Ask anyone, statistics or your female friends. These are the characters in a woman's life who are MOST likely to inflict abuse on a female, be it verbal, sexual, or emotional. It's nonsensical to search for solutions among the subgroup in society that is inflicting the harm in the first place. An armed, alert, and aware female traveling alone is much safer than a docile, naive, ignorant, fearful, or submissive female traveling with a male.

My Nishiki's First Ferry Ride

At midnight I loaded up my Nishiki to cross Lake Michigan on the ferry. She had a lovely time, nestled under the stairs by the other bikes. I was sleepy. I wanted to read and sleep on the ferry. Ever since I put the bumper sticker "This Vehicle Stops for Popcorn" on my Nishiki, I have felt compelled to get popcorn at every opportunity. I bought some popcorn for $2.50 and read from my book and tried to lay on the bench but I got horrible sleep. Flies kept landing on me and I wished I was wearing pants. When I got into Michigan, I was CRAZY desperate for sleep. I biked around until I found some nice pines on a lawn, tucked my bike away, and slept in the ivy in my sleeping bag. I woke up to a bunch of old people asking me if I was OK. This was not my preferred way to start the day.

Michigan Day 22 [ ] - Grand Rapids

Today I woke up at 11:30am. I ate McDonalds for breakfast. Two McChickens, a parfait, and an iced mocha. I added it up. It was enough calories for the whole day. This impressed me so much. I fixed my bike a little in the parking lot, and the grease refuses to wash off. I like the look. It was raining and windy when I left, and it was a hot rain and a hot wind. I biked east on Highway 10 and stopped at a post office to mail JD a book. The rain died down, and the clouds were giving occasional coverage, which I appreciated.

A cyclist who tours occasionally stopped me and gave me advice on where to bike. I took a lovely scenic route on a road surrounded by state park. I saw conifers and lots of fern and apple trees and horses and snakes. I stopped at a farm that sold honey and bought a big block of wax and some comb honey. The man asked me what I was going to use the wax for, and I said to wax the string I use for my books. I told him that if I found some Arnica I would like to make a balm to heal the bruises I keep accumulating as well. Honey makes me think of my sister.

By the end of the day, I decided that this was the loneliest day of my tour so far. I like playing more than biking alone. I don't really have any friends closer than DC, and DC feels far away. I got into Big Rapids late and camped in the cemetery. I ate ice cream for dinner and my favorite candy in the whole world for dessert. The candy was $3. The highlight of the night was falling asleep while reading.

Michigan, Day 23 Big Rapids- Mt. Pleasant

Today I woke up in the cemetery next to spiders and the sound of four weed-wackers. It sort of pissed me off, but then one of them came and talked to me. He was pretty cute so I forgave the noise. I got packed up and found coffee at an old person diner. These are my favorite diners. I mean, sometimes I'm in the mood for $3 coffee and fancy art, but not always. Sometimes they're cool, but sometimes they're hip and snobby. I chatted with some old ladies over breakfast and it was pleasant. I primped in the bathroom and felt good about that as well.

Mt. Pleasant is only 43 miles away, and I'm looking forward to biking through it. I want to find Shivansh and leave him a little note or present. This is my goal for the day. If only I knew how to spell his last name...

(A little backstory to my reader-Shivansh's one of the math professors from my first math research experience with the National Science Foundation. I didn't work with him on my project. In fact, we got off to a rocky start because the first thing I told him was how much I hated Linear Algebra, and later I learned that was what his focus was. But we definitely bonded. He is this really hilarious Indian mathematician. And He was the boy I loved academic advisor and mentor.)

I decided that I need something to look forward to before I get to DC. I think I'll visit Niagara Falls. The ladies at the diner highly recommended it. I won't go to Toronto unless I have a place to stay there ahead of time.

Hurray! I found Shivansh and I picked him a huge bouquet of wild flowers on the way! My Nishiki could barely hold them all, and I felt like a silly little hippie girl again, biking in a dress with wildflowers spilling off my bike. My Nishiki looked so adorable I took her picture. It was perfectly fitting considering where I was. If only I had long hippie hair and that green dress again I could pretend I was 19…

Slumber Party at Shivansh's!

Super fun!

Michigan Day 24: Shivansh's- Somewhere on Highway 57

I slept in today on a bed in the guest room in Shivansh basement. I read myself to sleep again, but only made it to page 7 of An Open Heart by the Dalai Lama. I think I get the gist. Compassion compassion. I probably don't get it, actually.

Shiv made me Costa Rican Coffee for breakfast and stirred the sugar in himself, which was cute. He also made me a sandwich, toasted the bread, and asked how much peanut butter I wanted. Shivand I watched "Slum Dog Millionaire" and I screamed a lot. He made me watch it though. I kept arguing that I was sensitive to violence, and he kept saying "but this really happens! Shivansh and MJ (his college-aged daughter) and I are just lounging around watching Home Improvement and my concern is that I will never get on the road today.

It's already 12:30. But whatever. What's another day to me now? I've plotted a route to keep me out of both Saginaw and Flint, and I'm proud that I found it. Cities are time sucks and I'm trying to get to Niagara Falls now. And I don't think there's any pressing need for me to go through Flint at this point in my trip.

The sweetest part of my trip today happened after I arrived in town and was setting up camp. A little boy on a bike wearing a helmet came up to me and asked:

"Have you seen my cousin and grandpa?"

"What do they look like?"

"Well, there's only two of them."

"Where were you the last time you saw them?"

"The baseball field"

“That would be a good place to wait for them to find you"

Then he hesitated, and I realized again that he was just a little boy. So I asked

"Do you want to wait here with me?"

"Yes"

"Do you want to help me set up my tent?"

"Well, I'm only seven and I've never done it before"

This practically broke my heart. I taught him how to set up my tent and he was loving it. I had him do nearly everything himself with just the necessary help from me. When it was up, he was so proud. Then his grandfather strolled up in the car and gave Tyler the standard 10 minute scolding and "I love you!" talk and chatted with me about my bike ride and such. As he pulled away, he was on the phone with his wife. I hear him say

"I found Tyler. And he made a girlfriend." I smiled.

Thinking about Tyler, his innocence and trust were so precious. We all had it once, and I can remember being little like that still. It is so tragic that we have to grow up in this world and lose it all. Tyler made me think of the kids at Twin Oaks, and the little boy that I took care of for two years. Winter. Winter Tree Star. The Star family was the most "F"ed-up family I have ever known. For one, his “father” was Mr. Charisma from Twin Oaks. If that gives you any idea of what this poor boy was up against. Winter’s world was so unstable he seemed to never feel secure and I remember how painfully we worked on building trust for two years, and toward the end, when no one was taking care of him, he came to my room frantic and crying and I read him Calvin and Hobbes and feed him corn from a can. He was holding his stuffed tiger, Roly Poly, and I tucked him under the covers.

That was the last time we spent together before I was taken to the hospital by his dad and everything changed for me. I remember holding him on my shoulders to watch the sunset over the pond through the woods. He's probably too big for that now, and I'm probably not allowed to visit even if I wanted. Now I wonder if his grown-up teeth are coming in healthy or if they are just as rotten as his baby teeth, and who in the family is taking responsibility for his health. I wonder if he still has wild tantrums when a new person is appointed to look after him and if he always submits to bully friends. There's no real way to know. I wish he was born with enough calcium in his body, that his parents gave him fluoride rinses even though they are hippie dumb fucks, and that his parents made the choice to sacrifice their own social lives to give him the basic security he needs to grow up healthy. He's seven now. Just like Tyler. And I guess that is why I'm thinking about him.

On the Arrival of Touring Bonus'

Just about two days ago and today I have begun to notice and enjoy the bonus' of extended bike touring. They are simple, but the shift has been acutely noticeable, so I feel it's worth sharing. The captain of my RAGBRAI team told me that about one month into touring you stop feeling pain and feel as if you could tour forever. For me, this has come right on time, at about 3.5 weeks. Now when I ride, I not only do not feel any pain or discomfort, but I feel a certain feeling of pleasure in my muscles pumping it. They like the work. I'm averaging about 17 miles per hour, which for me on my particular bike is a lot and has come as a huge surprise.

Biking is a lot more fun now. But other things are more fun too. The best and most surprising part of this whole shift is that I am now an eating machine! Not only CAN I eat everything I can see or want, but eating itself has completely changed. I'm not picky at all. I'm snacking on things like a whole block of cheese, an entire box of fruit snacks, a whole watermelon, three sandwiches, 1/4 gallon of whole milk in one sitting. My body just wants it all, and devours it all. It is SO fun to eat like this. I cannot overemphasize the previous statement. I'm building a ton of muscle, and I look super strong. I'm definitely not getting skinny hot like I had planned, but I'm not getting fat either, which is amazing. If you like to eat, I highly recommend bike touring. Also, if you're a girl and for whatever reasons have issues with cellulite, I also recommend bike touring.

Michigan day 25: Chesaning- Somewhere on 57

My day is just starting, and I am waking up later and later every day, sleeping more and more. I'll be on the road by noon if I'm lucky. I have nothing much to say except that though my body has broken through a brick wall, mentally and emotionally I'm beginning to suffer. Mornings are good- drinking coffee, waking up slowly. But night time is not, and I'm getting super depressed and lonely in a bad way as soon as the sun goes down. I'm on the phone for about an hour each night when I'd imagined I'd be making friends or reading or having adventures.

I want some drugs. My trip is shifting at this point. I don't have any friends between here and DC, and DC is not until Aug. 1st. I don't know anyone in Canada. I could stay at NASCO coops or warm showers, but I'm even lacking the motivation to make these things happen. I'm sick of coop kids anyway. The only people who get me and this experience at all are my friends who tour, and I don't have a ton of them. I'm feeling this sort of depressed recklessness right now, and I don't know what I'll do with it.

So far today I have managed to:

- Get some drugs
- Eat a ton of fruit
- Sign up at Warm Showers
- Mail JD a present for getting his Kindergarten shots.

R.I.P Frederick L. Forbush

Frederick L. Forbush. June 3rd, 1941- October 13, 1998.

I stayed by the grave of Frederic L. Forbush last night, and his brother came out and visited me. Well, him. And then me. First he sort of scared me because it was late and I was setting up camp. Then he kept driving by me and asking me questions. Finally, he came out and told me that he was visiting his brother's grave, and that his brother was a bike tourist as well. His dream was to tour through the 48 continental states on his bike. He made it East of the Mississpi, but not much further. He thought he had developed bronchitis along the way, but it was lung cancer.

On his tombstone is an etching of a man holding his bike pulling a trailor. I felt sort of honored that this guy shared his brother's story with me and he told me that seeing a bike tourist at his brother's grave made him feel happy, that it's probably the company his brother would have liked at his grave. This made me feel good. I thought that though I don't have any big dreams about bike touring, if I were to die before I make it out to Asia, I would like an etching of me scrubbing an elephant on my grave.

Michigan/Canada Day 26: Somewhere on 57- Canada (Hopefully)

Today I woke up to a person with a weedwacker telling me I'm not allowed to camp in the cemetary and to get out. Why didn't anyone tell me that cemetaries are full of loud and annoying weedwackers at 8am? Notably, criminals doing community service with poor manners? I would have liked to have been more pissed, but I was grateful for the alarm clock. I ate breakfast at THE CRAPPIEST diner I have ever been to. The coffee sucked. The hashbrowns came from a bag. My sunnyside up eggs had cooked yolks. And my toast choices were wheat or white. Luckily, I scored the breakfast for free, which made it all better. I keep considering writing a piece on how to get free things, especially food. But I'm wary of being so directly honest about the tactics one can employ after being called a "master manipulator."

I made a book today and mailed it, which was good. I'm about 40 miles away from Canada at this point, and it's noon. I would like to cross the border today for no particularly good reason- just to keep my trip moving and such. The wedding is a little over a month out. I'm excited to go to Canada today. I've never been. The border lady was nice and gave me a ride across the border. She very pretty. She warned me that Canadians are not very smart. Ha! In Canada, they took my tear gas away and searched my bike. It pissed me off. But then I went to the welcome center and had a merry time talking about everything related to Canada and the US with Brad, the young employee from Ottowa. Our discussion is posted below.

Canada vs. the US. Brad vs. Bok Choy:

Brad's reasons why Canada is better than the US and Bok Choy's counter arguments.

1. Canada is More Polite.

BC's Coutnter: Miss Manners. The US has Miss Manners' Guide to Everything.

2. Canada is less of a consumer culture
   BC: No counter
3. Colour, Favour, Flavour, Honour, and Zed (their word for the last letter in the alphabet).
   BC's response: Zee is still nice.
4. Monarchy! The Queen!
   BC's Response: We have The Daily Show. We had G.W. Bush for 8 years and his chimp-like public displays of stupidity sparked the Daily Show's existence.
5. Canada has more diverse political parties. Enough of this Democrat/Republican crap!
   BC's Response: Does Canada have a political underground like in the US?
6. Canada has a "No Fixed Address" option for nomadic or homeless persons to obtain library cards and vote.
   BC's Response: I would like to see the US follow this example.
7. Decrimilazed Pot.
   BC: Awesome.
8. Canadians go to Cuba.
   BC: No counter.
9. International Respect.
   BC: Does it piss you off that Americans sew Canadian flag patches on their packs?
   Brad: Yes
10. Pamela Anderson
    BC: No counter.

Canada Fun Facts (As told by Brad)

Chesterfield = Couch

Touque = Winter Hat

Chocolate Bar = Candy Bar

Coffee Crisp, Aero, Smarties

American Smarties = Rockets

Prostitution is legal in Canada, though not overly talked about.

B.C. Weed.

Universal Health Care--If you're gonna die, they take care of you.

CBC- Canadian Broadcasting System

"Canada's a pushover country"- Canadians don't protest

Canada, Day 27. Cemetary on Confederate Rd- Somewhere East of London

Last night I camped in another cemetery and fell asleep quickly. I wanted to sleep in and rest and read, but that is seriously impossible in this tiny tent. I slept in enough to get a proper late start and headed East toward London, my first big city along the way. It was 45 miles with no stops or towns getting there. I was officially blistering in the scorching sun. I was biking through farm country.

I saw:

- A brilliant cabbage patch unlike any I had ever seen before
- Strange Hay Bales
- Corn
- Soybeans
- Two Llamas with their own stream and bridge to play on.
- A baby calf and her momma eating her placenta and shaking it around with her teeth.

I ran out of water and some farmers gave me more.

I got so weak and tired on the way that I had to pull over to refuel. This meant eating my bag food, which was less than pleasant. I put some electrolyte powder in my bottles and regretted the nastiness. When I made it to London, I bought lots of food, including brie, which I was unable to find at all in Michigan. I have been eating a container of blueberries everyday. I drank a whole container of apple juice in one gulp, which felt amazing. Then I went to a store and scored an amazing hikers coat for the mountains which I feel great about.

Things that I don't like about Canada is that lots of places don't take plastic. Things that I do like is how the people say "about."

Canada Day 28: Woodstock

Today I took my day of rest in Woodstock, Ontario. It was the first town in Canada that I have liked a lot and I was glad to stay there. I slept in, consumed fancy coffee, read, and hiked. I took a bath with baby wipes and tried to clean up. I did what I could. A lady at the drug store gave me some stuff I wanted for free, and I scored* sweet rose tinted sunglasses. They are the the best pair of sunglasses I have ever owned. I am turning into a bike. I washed the grease off my legs with dishsoap and my chain toothbrush. I came to realize that I left my camera in Michigan, which is sad.

The highlight of my day was the coconut rice I had at this strangely cool Thai restaurant and the med student I met there. Her name was Samantha and she had a cool kid and was a single mom rocking it in Med school like nobody's business. I liked her. We talked about corn politics, medicine, scuba diving, swimming with sharks, communes, organics, farming, men, dealing with men, medical school, logic, comparative psychiatry, and books we liked. I spent the rest of the night napping and reading in my tent. I talked to a boy on the phone and felt weird during and after the conversation. *Dad, feel free to freak out.

Canada Day 29: Woodstock-Brantford

I set out from Woodstock early and refreshed, and onto a trail toward Niagara Falls. I started to get hungry as the trail passed through a town. I saw some people sitting on a bench and asked them what town I was in. Brantford. I asked them where I could get food, and a guy pointed toward a Wendy's hidden behind a tall building. He told me to bring him back a hamburger when I came back.

So I took the opportunity to notice him. He was Native North American, publicly drinking, about 40ish, and he was wearing dirty work clothes. He was missing several teeth. His two friends were a little older looking and in power scooters, also drinking and also Native North American. So I told the guy that I would bring him back a burger. I got a whole bunch of food and came back and he was so happy and sweet. He made room for me on the bench. I gave him his burger and he gave it to his 'cousin,' as he called her. Her name was Sandra.

I needed to sit and eat regardless of my company, and I watched Kent and Sandra's banter as they bickered over silly things, like how Sandra wanted his lighter and his hat. Sandra kept complaining about how much her butt hurt. Then she pointed to a plastic bag stuck in a tree and made us all look and she laughed really hard. It was fun, and I wanted to hang out with them.

I drank and smoked cigarettes and we all got sort of drunk, though Kent was far ahead of everyone. We seemed to be in scooter central and Kent seemed to be the life of the social club, even though he didn't have a scooter. He was friends with everyone. Everyone passing by was waving at him. So then this thin, feeble old man scoots by to cross the bridge. He looked about 90 years old. And Kent yells "Hey Jeronimoooo!" So I yell it too. And then Sandra yells it. He looks up a little bit and gives us a feeble and meek smile from his toothless mouth and crosses the bridge, spine collapsed forward on his little vehicle. I asked Kent how he knew him and he said "I've never seen that guy in my life."

I asked them questions about the Canadian government and I heard Sandra's abridged version of her shit early life. How she was taken from her mother at age 10 and put in foster care, forced to learn English and stripped of her Native Language. How she lost her entire family and was raped in her teens and contracted a venereal desease and became sterile, though she didn't know it at the time. How she moved to Toronto and got hooked on Heroine and got into knife fights in bathrooms and what she did for money. She told me about the time she spent in jail. She told me about how she found her little brother and he then took after her and then over-dosed on China White.

Kent was a Mohawk, and when he started telling his story he just collapsed into himself, sobbing and speaking incoherently between breaths. Sandra kept telling me he was the nicest guy when he was sober, that everybody loved him. I showered at Sandra's and she showed me things. Pictures of her brother. She confessed that she didn't need her scooter, but she got it for free and it was now her taxi. But that the other day she fell in a hole and her whole scooter tipped over. That was why her butt hurt. She's suing the city. I was in her bathroom talking on the phone and she told me we were going out, right now. She got on her scooter and I followed her on my bike all around the city.

It was beyond silly- navigating on a bike the way a scooter does. She took me to the Casino and the security people were assholes to me. They told me my passport was not authentic and I said as a joke mostly to myself but outloud "Wouldn't it be funny if my passport could get me into the country but not into the casino?" The manager just flipped out and said "Well we don't know that. We don't know this got you into the country" and I just retorted "You don't have to tell me everything you don't know. I'm well aware it's a lot." It was just this super bitchy uncensored thing I said because I hate everyone who looks at my passport and I'd been drinking. And the boy next to her just started laughing and she said "Alright, it checks out."

Sandra played the slots and had all these silly rules for which machines to pick and all that. She rubbed the screen just so before her plays. She won

$20 though. I played blackjack and won $7.50. Then I got really sick and sat outside until Sandra was done, which was like forever. We scooted around town and enjoyed it. We went to a big fountain and splashed around and she was constantly ducking her head and scooting really fast to avoid talking to people.

She had a story for everyone in town and why they sucked. It seemed no one was on her good side. I was afraid to cross her, but she reassured me that she liked me. I sort of enjoyed being with someone with a harsher, more dominant personality than my own and following her like a puppy. I never had to take responsibility for entertaining myself. She was constantly just cracking me up and taking me places. I got distracted on my bike by a cute boy and Sandra just kept zipping by around town. I assumed she'd wait up for me, but she didn't.

How I ended up both finding her apartement building, getting through the door, and finding her room when I didn't know her last name was a series of obstacles that I enjoyed overcoming, one by one. We stayed up late and she told me all her wild stories from Toronto. Like the time she slashed the tits of a chick who was messing with her man in a knife fight in a bar and then just walked out like it was no big deal. She made me promise her never to go there by myself. This now is the second person who has made me promise not to go to Toronto. She told me about her love scandals that still occurred in her little building for older people. So silly. So fun. We ate pizza and I slept on her couch, listening to really good music with the lights one. I love sleeping with the lights on to music.

Canada Day 30: 127 Missed Waterfalls/Ridge Road

Today I missed 127 waterfalls. That was going to be the theme of the day and the title of my entry. My day started with a warm embrace from Sandra and breakfast. Sandra insisted that I take her address and number and call and write her. She told me she wanted to give me things, and she gave me the second most beautiful necklace I have ever seen. She gave me a beautiful pendant as well. She kept hugging me until I left. I think she liked having someone to listen to her life story. And she was happy because she finally scored some pain pills.

I set off on the trail and ran out of water, as is usual. I stopped at a little organic CSA farm and asked for water and chatted with the people. A super cute and hot farm boy filled my bottles and everyone told me while he was gone that he has biked all over Australia, Canada, and Asia. He came back with a bunch of trail maps and gave me directions toward Hamilton, the next big city the trail would be going to. It supposedly was famous for having the highest concentration of waterfalls in one area. The farm girls and the boy argued as to how many waterfalls there actually were, and it ranged from 87-129. I believed the girl who claimed there to be 127.

I was excited. I wanted to go swimming and take my Nishiki under her first waterfall. If I had my camera I would have taken cute pictures of her all wet and silly. But it would be fun regardless. The trail was a bit wonky and cut off and restarted quite a bit. The boy talked a lot about the "escarpment" and how I would have to navigate around it and how this was tricky. I didn't really know what that was, but I just thought "whatever, I'll figure it out"

As I was leaving, he looked at my bike and told me he was jealous of me. That I was so free and he was tied to the land. As I biked away with fresh farm water, I realized I was hungry and that I was out of bike food. I ran into an apple tree, a blackberry patch, and some cucumbers a farmer set out for the taking. It really hit the spot. The trail ended in downtown Hamilton, a big city of 1/2 a million people. I systematically attempted to get back on the trail at all of its start spots again and was unsuccessful.

Many people stopped to help me, and several times they made reference to "climbing the mountain." I ignored this, as there were no mountains in sight. After I had missed all the trail entrances in the city, my last resort was to get on a very major road to get to the road the trail merged onto: Ridge Road. I got on the highway and noticed that I had to go uphill over a bridge and there was no shoulder. This was seriously going to suck, and I prepared for angy honking and pissed off cars.

As I biked along the bridge, I realized I was not going over water but that the highway kept winding and getting steeper. I got in my lowest gear and went as slow as I have ever gone. My legs cashed out and my butt started taking the slack. But then my butt maxed out and my lower back started carrying the load. I had never biked a steeper incline on my Nishiki. I began to realize that I was climbing the mountain. It appeared to have no end. About 15 minutes into the climb, the storm that had been looming all day released its rain and my climb of doom became a drenched one.

I found it only fitting. 127 missed waterfalls and an endless climb in a storm on a busy highway with splashing semis. I climbed for at least 30 minutes, I swear. I didn't bother to put on my rain gear. What good was comfort now? When I made it to Ridge Road, I saw the bike trail I had missed winding up and though the vineyards. I thought about how much I would have loved to bike that trail, and considered backtracking through the trail toward the waterfalls. But I went on. I had missed it and that was that. The storm ended just as I properly entered Ridge Road.

As the rain let up, the clouds to the South still held dark and heavy while the clouds to the north were white and light. Ridge Road. was right between them, and the atmospheric pressure gave both the feeling of the magic before the storm and after the storm. There was fruit everywhere. Pear orchards and vineyards and apple trees. The fruit hung over the road in such a way that you could bike just right underneath them and pick whatever you wished. I noticed to the North through the trees that I was high above the city and the view was breathtaking. I loved it. I saw the lake too, and wondered why I hadn't taken a swim. The view reminded me of Pest from the Buda side and the light up crosses tucked in the trees at the edge of the mountain reminded of the mountains in Switzerland. I hadn't realized how big the city was until I was up high.

To my left was the city, to my right was friut and trees and vineyards, and directly in front of me, arching over Ridge Road, was a huge double rainbow. I was in a fantasy world and I didn't know where to look. It was all too good. Ridge road is my most favorite place in Canada. It took me to a nature park where I was hoping to camp. Once again I thought I had found the trail and it took me into the woods and my Nishiki almost skidded down a cliff. The view from the cliffs were great, but it was a twisted trail of doom. Beamer is it's name. Don't bike the Beamer Trail off Ridge Rd., whatever you do. You might lose your bike.

I made it out alive and got on Ridge Road again, headed East. I was out of water and saw a little rugby recreation center. It was a boys club, but the boys were all busy playing in the field so I parked my bike and went in in search of water. I found it. And was also found by the team, demanding an explanation. They can run pretty quickly...

In the end, I made a call at one of those Canadian gas stations that is also a head shop and when I was off the phone it was dark. Like totally dark. So I just pulled behind the church across the street and threw down my tent. I read a little bit and slept pretty well. I wasn't cold at all in the night.

Canada Day 31: Grimsby - Queenston

Not too much about this day. I biked down the mountain in search of food and scored a sweet Hello Kitty head for the rubber skeleton that has been protecting me during my journey. Then I headed back on Ridge Road toward Niagara Falls. I biked until I reached the river and decided to take it easy and camp early. On the way I saw the bus I want. It's a 4 window double decker diner bus. The bottom is a fry kitchen and the top is eating seating. I called the guy, but had no luck reaching him.

I ended in Queenston, which is a super touristy, bed-and-breakfasty, old money kind of town and it was really nice. There were flowers everywhere and big beautiful houses and white picket fences. I camped on Princess Road behind a church and strolled down to the river and read. I read for about three hours and was pleased. If I could give touring cyclists only three pieces of advice, it would be:

1. bring bug repellent
2. pack baby-wipes
3. bring a really really good book

There was a concrete bench seated over the Niagara River and the view was lovely. I could see New York and it was noisy with music. I didn't mind too much. At this point in my tour the highlight of my day is crawling into my tent and reading. I'm setting up camp earlier and earlier.

Canada Day 32: How I saw Niagara Falls

Today I slept in and began my search for a gas station. I was going to have packet oatmeal for breakfast and spend very little money today. There wasn't much in sight beyond residential housing, so I stopped in on a bed and breakfast and asked for directions. I thought I was going to walk into the office, but it was the kitchen/restaurant. I asked the lady my question, and she told me that there wasn't a gas station in town. I needed breakfast to take my medicine. I asked if the restaurant was for guests only, and she said yes, but that she would make me something. Her husband was opposed to this, and insisted that she alone serve me.

I had coffee in a little cup and warm cream that was sitting on the table. She brought me cereal with milk, a glass of milk and orange juice, and toast. She kept calling me "the little girl" to her husband, who was doing most of the cooking. "And make some toast for the little girl" "The little girl needs more coffee" The ladies in the B&B became quite chatty with me when they heard I was biking and I liked it. It seems I had missed the butterfly garden and I was sad about this. The old lady showed me the bike path to Niagara Falls and I really appreciated that. She charged me very little for my food and filled up my bottles.

A biker came in just as I was leaving and asked: "Are you climbing or descending?"

"Climbing"

"Have fun"

It wasn't that bad. The mountain to Ridge Road was way worse. The trail seemed to be yet another wonderland. Not like Ridge Road, but one very intentionally created by humans for beauty. There were flowers everywhere and I became a little confused as to why the trail was so beautiful until I realized it cut through the botanical gardens. The trail followed the river, and I liked this because I always knew where I was.

I saw a silly clock that was huge and covered in flowers. There was a sign that said "Keep of the Clock" I was excited to see the falls, and decided to see them via helicopter. They let me sit with the pilot and our headsets were connected so we could chat up in the air. I told everyone my sob story about losing my camera and the guy told me I could have some pictures for free. That's a savings of $25 Canadian per picture. This made me happy. Yah, I didn't get my dream photo of me and my Nishiki by the falls, but I got a pretty sweet one of me wearing these super cool glasses and headsets in a rainbow helicopter.

My goals for the day were to get to The States today and figure out my route. I crossed over the Rainbow Bridge over the Niagara River on my little Nishiki and I swear I saw a huge rainbow on the New York side, welcoming us in. The toll was $.50 for a bike. The town of Niagara was dizzying and I wanted out fast. I remembered that some friends of mine recommended the Eerie Canal Bike Path, and I set out to find it. I headed out east on 31 until I came to the town of Lockport.

I had a good hour and a half of cycling left in me and in the day, but I did not know where the bike trail was. A storm was looming and I was eager to find the trail and set up camp. I stopped at a house and asked for water and directions. I got both and a steak dinner, conversation with a former bike racer and his cool fiancee, and a whole ginormous camper to myself. There was actually a tornado watch. I had already eaten a hot dog and two packets of trail mix at the gas station, but eating at the table, I was a machine. The bike racer thought this was really funny, that it reminded him of his racing days.

They kept piling on food to see if I could still eat, and it was nice because it extended our social time by a nice half an hour. I ate two full dinners of steak, potatoes, and corn. I wanted to show off my Nishiki to the guy, and he liked it. He always rode on some crazy expensive Bianchi racing bike. I had a Bianchi in Hungary, and a really cool Schwinn that had the exact birthday as me in Iowa City, and I swore for a long time that I was Bike E for life. Still, no bike has ever been so great as my little blue women's Nishiki Century. Sometimes, I just burst with pride that my little $10 garage sale bicycle has come this far- from atrophying inside of an old barn to carrying all our stuff and taking us all over the country and more. She rode all the way across Illinois with a broken spoke and barely complained. And now she's cruising over the Rainbow bridge in high style.

The camper was SO MUCH FUN! It was huge and awesome. I asked the guy how much it cost him, and he said 10K. I said "Whatever, these are like $70,000." He said "Yah, new they are. But I got mine used and rebuilt the engine." I sat in the driver's seat and play drove for a while and lounged on the couch and read for a long time. The storm was raging and the camper had perfect ventilation. I slept in this sweet bed and I opened all the windows until it got really cold and curled up under the blankets. Somehow, I didn't really get wet. That's one of my favorite things about the cold. Sleeping warm in the cold.

Let Your Life Speak. There are a Thousand Ways to Kneel and Kiss the Earth-Rumi

I indulged and read some Sufi poetry and was moved by a line by Rumi. I decided that I wanted kneel and kiss the earth. So I did. And then I decided I wanted to do it 1000 times. So I began a new daily practice.

Kiss [0]

Crawling out of my tent at 11 o'clock p.m. in Upper New York State with my light turned off to avoid the mosquitoes, skin damp from the roof of my tent bearing down on my legs and the slick rainwater on damp ground.

The Kiss.

Shocked by the sweetness of wet grass.

Kiss [1]

Bearing down toward compact earth and green, my face falls into a delicate valley of 3-leaved clovers and young honeysuckle wearing stripes of pink I haven't seen in years.

The Kiss.

Tasteless and mossy.

Kiss [2]

My torso shivering like my body had forgotten what it was like to be cold, my knees fall onto a thick and untamed grass, the kind my father would have destroyed with his store-bought poisons shooting from a spray pump. A tiny cricket jumps to an unmarked tomb and I follow it to a rock giving the illusion of smoothness, its discolored streaks of greys and tans washing over it like turbulent waves at high sea on a dark and overcast morning- my face smothered full force into this storm of thick grass.

The Kiss.

Lingering.

Leaving.

Returning again for another while slugs make their way to one another, sliming their paths over our tomb.

New York, Day 36

After shivering in damp tents for three days now, I have a proper cold. An old lady gave me piles of elderberry and I am sucking on zinc against her warnings. Here in New York, I am always cold. Always damp. I wish for a warm brown hat with ear flappys and braided dangles down past my shoulders and wool mittens for sleepy time and a tarp for under my tent and a warmer sleep bag.

I can bear the cold, but I don't like being sick. My lungs are hurty and I have a cough. The kind where you suppress it because once you start, you cough more than you can bear. I mailed my hiking coat home just a few days ago, and now more than ever I wish I had her for sleeping. I see Ithaca today, and I hope to get out of NY fast fast fast.

I did make it out of NY pretty fast. It's amazing what you can do when you hit the road by 7:30a and stay on highways. I invested in my health and some sweet gear, which include

- A tarp for under my tent (shaped EXACTLY like my Walrus tent!)
- This cool liner for my sleeping bag that makes it 15 degrees warmer. (Awesome)
- Spray to make my tent more water and UV resistant.

I told the guy I was a student and got 15% off. And I am. But still, all in all this stuff was way out of my price range and money is getting tight. But I mean, when am I going to get well but in the night? I saw a Buzz Lightyear action figure on a chair with a "free" sign taped to it. I wanted to attach him to my bike to ward off aliens. But there is so much shit on my bike at this point, I didn't even know where to put him.

On my bike:

- A rubber skeleton with a hello- kitty doll stuffed inside, head showing
- Sunflowers on the front left pannier

- A pelt atop the stuff bundled to my back rack
- A Pocahontas lunchbox dangling over my back tire

I mean, where would I put Buzz?

Kiss [3]

The sun pours though my tent, burning my eyes open and awake when every part of my body protests awakeness. Awareness. Motion. My aching middle back. My right shoulder. My upper gums.

Now, spilling out, I walk toward the old pine that has been pruned so many times its scars bleed resin stains of a deep and toxic green.

I kneel before an exposed root into a tiny world of fractal geometry on green surfaces and little baby trees, proudly displaying their unproportionally large three and perfect leaves.

The Kiss.

Full and rough like early morning on unshaved chin.

PA: Day 37: Pneumonia.

Pennsylvania has Mountains! I camped on private property. Say it was dumb, but if you had seen it, you would not have resisted as well. Anyway, I was awakened in the night with flashlights, kicks on my tent, and threats to call the police. I silenced myself, and thought "What would Dale Carnegie do?" [Note to my reader: I read <u>How to Win Friends and Influence People</u> in preparation for my ride]

I followed the instructions of his book very carefully, and got the man to move from kicking my tent to calling me "buddy" to offering me a shower in the morning. It was a success, and I was surprised I got away with it. The shower was super nice and I used little kid lice shampoo. I considered using my own, then thought: "Just to be on the safe side..." I was warm that night.

My tent was dry and my liner made me so warm I was actually HOT for a while. I gave some thought to the fact that I read, almost exclusively, non-fiction and poetry while I aspire to write a novel. No wonder I am struggling to develop my characters. I made the decision a few days ago to read a fiction for every non-fiction I read, with poetry unrestricted. Ok, what am I saying? I'm trying to say that I'm reading <u>Wuthering Heights</u>. Just don't make fun of me for this, OK?

Oh yah, so I have Pneumonia. After feeling like shit and crying on my bike soon after my ride, I went to a doctor in the nearest town. I tried eating to feel better, but it just made me want to barf. He thought I was pregnant. The nurse thought I was malnourished. But my urine and a stethescope told them I have a really bad infection in my lungs. Everyone felt sorry for me.

The doctor thought I was dumb. Like cognitively deficient for not having a job and riding my bike alone. They gave me my visit for free and my drugs for five dollars. The nurse wheeled in my bike to the office and watched it while I ran errands (this one included). I can't have prolonged sun exposure on my anti-biotics and I'll probably be staying in a church for a while. My drugs last for seven days. I'm really not that upset. I need a good excuse to get some of my work done, anyhow.

I'm sad because my sister and I are not mutually happy over a boy, and this is the most divisive thing that can enter a relationship like ours. We both have boy-weakness'. And we're both super co-dependant on one another. And this is just so silly, because all our dialogues are happening over facebook.

PA: Day 38: My dank motel and more.

So some things are sweet right now and some things are not.

Not Sweet: Pneumonia.

Sweet: Anti-biotics for $5.

Not sweet: Intense Sun-burn risk on said anti-biotics.

Sweet: Free Motel Room.

Not Sweet: Black mold in the shower.

Sweet: Free Food at the Lodge.

Not Sweet: Old lady that serves you and the salt that doesn't come out of the shaker.

Sweet: Lovely town of Dushore, PA

Not Sweet: 10 mile climb up the mountain toward said town.

Sweet: Peach pie with ice-cream.

Not Sweet: Feeling freezing all the time.

Sweet: Unlimited internet usage at the library.

Not Sweet: Ripped and torn panniers.

Sweet: Super cool fabric for mending my panniers...This list could go on.

I am in Dushore, Pennsylvania. And it already feels like home to me. I practically know everyone in town, simply from visiting the doctor, nurse, chatting with the ladies at the variety store, eating peach pie and praising the baker, and hanging out at the library. There are only 640 people in this town. I swear I'm the only one with a bike here and when I left the variety store full on peach pie carrying new fabric and patches for my panniers, my nurse came up to me and just gave me a big hug.

So this is where I live right now: in the land of pie and libraries and nurses that love you and hug you and free food and dank mountain air and sick lungs. If things never changed I wouldn't complain much. So I guess I'll stay for a bit.

Kiss [4]

Throwing on clothes and escaping my nakedness under the worn and course sheets of my dank motel, my lungs still feel like pneumonia and my mouth tastes like a hangover and a bad one-night-stand, even though I'm sober and alone.

Stepping out from my room, I press my bare soles on the gravel as they take me toward a stack of drying firewood fifteen feet wide and taller than I, supported between three naked and thin oaks.

As I draw near, I see damp Turkey Tail mushrooms everywhere and I kiss them ravenously. I kneel down.

The Kiss.

Gritty.

Kiss [5]

Turning my locks 90 degrees East and swinging the door open I feel the shock of brisk and damp mountain air on my shoulders, in my lungs, through my sheet.

Quickly, walking barefoot over compact soil, I pass the old picnic table carrying cinder blocks holding up a pile of PVC pipes toward an old conifer.

It is covered in yellowy-green patches of some lifeform I cannot identify, but which has brilliantly developed tiny surface structures which I have studied in school. I kiss a few patches, noticing they grow atop browner, deader looking patches beneath them. I bow down.

The Kiss.

Quick and cold.

PA: Day 39, Pneumonia: Day 3.

I had a rough night. It was a mix between feeling sad, lonely, angry, misunderstood, disrespected, and rejected. I need to stop making calls to my dad. But I got a lot of good writing out of it, but I don't think it's the kind of stuff for this audience. It's good. But it's not for this forum, I suppose. I get sick of writing narratives, but I guess it's good practice.

I walked into the Pine Tavern today for breakfast and a woman nearly accosted me before I could sit down. "Are you the biker?" "Are you in room 8?" She had me sit at the bar with her, which I didn't care for because I wanted to work on my sewing while I waited for my food. And she wanted to talk to me, which again, I didn't care for because it was morning.

But now I believe I have met one of the most wonderful women in my life, and we connected like old girlfriends in a matter of a few minutes. She was probably in her late 30's, but her skin was tight and dark and her jaw was, well exotic. I asked what she was and she said one part Cicilian and one part Sauk Indian with a little Eastern Europian mutt in her, and that explained it sufficiently to me.

We talked about boys and relationships and our favorite painters and the mediums we were into right now and how it felt when we were doing our art and not apologizing for all the rest we weren't doing. I told her I haven't been painting so much as making books, and I didn't understand why such an obscure craft has me so captivated and she told me to jump through any window I ever get a chance to see open up to me and don't delay.

And she told me to stop taking my medicine. Her name was Valerie Anne. She left to go clean rooms and I moved to a table to eat "The Usual"- hot cocoa, a large glass of orange juice, a large green tea, and garlic homefries. I worked on my mending and the old lady who runs the place told me all sorts of stories about how she had to hem up her dresses in secret when her grandma wanted them below her knees and how she responds to the rude little comments her husband makes about her clothes. She's 73. I didn't really care to hear, but she seemed to want to tell.

She told me so many little things and I just nodded from my sewing every so often, sipping my cocoa. She was the cook today, and her homefries were better than the others'. When I got up to pour coffee into my cup, as everyone does, she insisted on taking it from me and filling it herself, when I was right there. And then she told me she was going into town and could pick me up whatever I needed.

"Like what?" I asked.

"Pizza? A sub sandwhich? I have turkey in the fridge though, and I can make you a hoagie..."

"I'll just come back to the restaurant for lunch."

It didn't make sense. But I guess it doesn't have to. I watched old movies in my room and drank juice and took a nap and then biked to the library, 10 miles uphill in the mountains. And tonight I'll pack up and prepare for the road again tomorrow.

Kiss [6]

Walking briskly in stride to the last place behind the parking lot I have yet to kiss, I squat down toward an old phone pole beginning to decompose. It is clothed in rags which have been drying in the damp mountain air for days now, weeks I suspect. Pulling forward, I see tints and shades and layers of brown that I'd never hear about in art school- secret shades only the anthropology students and their teachers knew. Still, I want to meet them all too.

The Kiss.

Another indescribable.

PA Day 40: My Little Mountain Town

I spent the day in my little mountain village today. It wasn't raining by mountain standards, but it's always misty up here. Valerie hugged me vigorously and stopped traffic behind her when she saw me on the street. I biked 10 miles to my little village to talk on the phone. $20 in phone cards today, sold to me in $10 increments. My mountain village has flowers everywhere and chimes tucked up high and the little Shoppe with peach pie. My little mountain library has silly little librarians that giggle so loud that I can barely type. I don't want to leave.

PA Day 41

I'm sick of biking.

Kiss [7]

Tucked in the mountains, in a cornfield in central PA, burns a single rogue stalk. Standing 18 or more inches above the rest, its reds and oranges effortlessly command me to throw my bike off the shoulder and wade into the jungle of the field toward it. Pulling the top down toward my head, I see its ears heaving in fullness away from the giant stalk while the others around it are still growing. I do not know if I will break it.

The Kiss.

Bursting.

PA DAY 42

My sleep has improved from cold and wet to simply cold. It helps me get on the road earlier. But I don't fall asleep quickly and I'm too cold to read. Biking in the mountains, is, well..., an experience. If I could break down this part of the PA Appalachian Mountains, I would say it's:

- 1 part downhill
- 2 parts "relatively flat"
- 7 parts uphill.

Calculating distance is becoming confusing. I biked all day pretty hard and I supposedly only made 55ish miles according to my map. But this confuses me, and I'm not sure if my map calculates distance as the crow flies or not.

Really going down a mountain has required me to get off the shoulders or right of the lane and into the lane properly. This is scary, because the path is not flat. It's all curvy, so vehicles don't have a lot of time to see me. But then I came to realize that when I'm really flying down, I'm going about the speed of traffic anyway. I'm only a few days from DC, with my frind from Twin Oaks in her little cottage on the farm she loves to much. I can't wait to show her my awesome new hair.

Kiss [8]

Perched on a hill, past the church and the 'closed due to breaking tombstones' cemetery, I wake up and see the cross below. Large and wooden, with benches around it, it sits near a tiny pond that most surely is used for baptisms.

Now, walking toward the sun, it seems I've found the one spot in the whole earth without bugs or dew. Kneeling before a patch of grass covered in its own decomposing clippings, my face falls into the earthy and musky smell of it all.

The Kiss.

Short. With remnants sticking to my chapstick.

PA: Day 43. How I ate a crab.

Today I learned how to eat a crab. But before that happened I:

- Woke up freezing again.
- Ate breakfast at a truckstop.
- Biked a lot.
- Stumbled into the town of Hershey, PA on Chocolate Ave.
- Passed the Cocoa-Plex Movie Theater on the way out of town.
- Biked some more.
- Swore I wouldn't spend any more money on food for the day.
- Saw a crab-shack.
- Pulled over.

So I walk in and I sit. A girl covers my table and the floor in newspapers, and hands me a wooden spiked mallet, a knife, and a plastic bucket. This seemed so silly, as usually I just get a little metal crunching tool. But that is because, being from the Midwest, I only have eaten crab legs. Silly, it's just what I expect when I order crab. So when she brought out this huge tray with six whole red sort of big crabs, I was just shocked. They still had their eyes. I knew they wouldn't pinch me. And I was scared to grab the first one. But I did. After looking at it, I decided I'd better just go ahead and whack it. I cracked open the body and looked inside. There were strange grey nodes and slimy yellowy gunk near the face and then "normal"-ish crab meat as well.

I started with the nodes, and they were sort of rubbery and icky. Then I went for the regular crab meat but the nasty yellow stuff was all over it. Then I just went for the legs. I needed to know if the yellowy stuff was something the cook put in or if it was part of the crab. Like it should matter, but it did. I asked the waitress and she told me she'd be right back. A lady nearby overheard me and asked me if she could show me how to eat a crab. I said yes. She showed me a special 'key' at the bottom that you lift up and the shell comes off. The nodes were the lungs of the crab, and she said most people did not eat them. The yellow stuff was indeed part of the crab and referred to as "the mustard." Some people ate it, some people didn't.

Then some real southern girl came out from the kitchen and started giving me lessons on how to eat a crab, and she was super condescending. She showed me the key trick, and then told me not to eat the lungs because they were poisonous. So I just react to this. I gasped a really loud gasp which bordered on a reverse scream. I told her I ate some.

She said "Well don't. They're poisonous."

I said "Well no one told me!"

I asked her what I should do- if I should call poison control. I had eaten two sets of lungs. She didn't know. I asked her if she had ever known of anyone surviving eating the lung. She said she'd never known of anyone to eat the lung before. All she seemed to know was that they were poisonous. I felt really frustrated that:

1. No one had warned me
2. No one seemed to know what to do

Everyone around seemed to think it wasn't a big deal, but agreed that it was common knowledge that crab lungs were poisonous. What did that mean- "poisonous"? Are they toxic in large doses? Are they deadly? Are they simply difficult to digest? There didn't really seem to be anything I could do at this point. I didn't have a phone to call poison control and it was past dark on a highway between towns. So I decided to just sit back and focus on eating more crab. I was getting better at it, and while I was eating, I noticed that everyone in the crab-shack was fat. Like actually and properly fat, eating crab ravenously with newspaper hanging from their collars. I was eating just as ravenously and I didn't even have the manners to cover myself in paper.

I did not like this.

So then a while later the cook comes out and announces to the whole back half of the shack that crab lungs are indeed NOT "poisonous"-that they are merely bitter and undesirable to eat. The room was in shock. Everyone started whispering "But my father always told me not to eat them!", etc. I felt relieved knowing that someone knowledgeable worked in the shack.

HOW TO COOK CRAB: Boil it whole. Cover in Old Bay.

HOW TO EAT CRAB: Lift up the "key" underneath and open up the shell with your thumb.

I camped behind a little motel on the highway and used their bathroom. I felt paranoid about eating crab in that fat-shack so I broke down and looked at myself in the mirror naked.

Report: I am not getting fat.

Washington, DC: Right on Time

All that matters about today is that it ended with my friend from Twin Oaks and me tucked up in her cottage, drinking fruit wine. The day was eventful and full and I was pretty stoned on something that runs sort of like adrenaline in the body during the last 30 miles or so. I still can't believe I biked on Route 7. My catsuit went from black panther to snow leopard and my skin was super salty.

One thing that was funny was how my friend from Twin Oaks was taking my appearance.

She kept repeating: “Choy. You’re blonde. And tan” like she was trying to explain something to me I didn’t already know. It was my friend’s first night in her adorable blue cottage and we spent the night there together, gossiping and whatnot. Watching Gregg Araki films on VHS. And my Nishiki had taken me there just on time.

Kiss [9]

Sitting atop Blueberry Hill, my joints hurt too much to kneel. My feet hurt too much to move me. So I just put my face into the yellow daisy plant to rest, trying to get the strength to get up and kneel properly.

The Kiss.

Tiny Kisses.

Post Tour, Day 1: Sandwiched by Babes

Days on the farm are full. My friend from Twin Oaks' cottage is next to the hen house, which means waking up at 5 am. Work starts at 7am. I have never worked on a CSA farm, and filling the orders was a bit stressful. I think I did a good job helping. My Keens are out of commission. Along with all four of my panniers. And my air mattress in the worst way. And my feet. I don't know exactly what to do with them. I might see a doctor in the city, but I doubt that's what they need. I sprained my big toe in a bike accident 3 days ago, but it's not just my right foot that's hurting. I think they've taken a lot of neglect on this ride. I think they need some TLC.

I've always worked barefoot on farms except when using shovels. It's a natural thing for me- I like the feeling. This is the only time they don't hurt- when I'm walking around barefoot on the farm. Inside, I feel like an old lady whining about her aches and pain.

My friend's coworker and I got off to a rocky start when I thought he was being disrespectful toward my Nishiki over an off-handed comment he made. He also told me to put on shoes when he saw me walking up to the cottage. This pissed me off, as I'm not accustomed to taking orders from strange men. We had an interaction about it. The result was him handing me $20. This is the fourth time a strange man has handed me $20 on my trip. Directly to me, in person. My friend's identical twin sister bought me a pair of moccasins with it. My feet hate them. Being with the twins is super fun. When we ride around on the golf cart, They yell "Sandwiched by Babes" for everyone to hear.

Washington, DC

I stayed with my friend on her farm and by chance I got a day job helping a guy sell his produce at farmer's market and it paid cash daily. This was utterly fantastic, and I was able to buy a gorgeous vintage black evening gown and a string of pearls for the wedding. The wedding was near, and I was feeling ever more confident that I was going to make it on time.

Visiting Jason Shark

After a nice time resting and playing in DC, it was time to head on my way toward Boone, NC which was less than 450 miles away, and I had over two weeks left to make it. I had planned to stop and visit an old boyfriend, Jason Shark, who I had dated after I broke up with the man with the white gloves. He lived at a small intentional community near Twin Oaks. My friend from Twin Oaks drove me to meet him along with a handful of people from Twin Oaks who missed me and wanted to see me.

I had a weird energy when I saw everyone. I can't really explain it. Maybe everyone was interested in my trip, but deep down I felt self-conscious and thought maybe everyone wanted to see for themselves just how "crazy" I was. I remember trying to cover up my nervousness by playing song after song on my ukulele. Jason later told me that he could tell I was uncomfortable.

It was a bit strange staying at this small community. There were a bunch of guys who lived there who I had history with from my time at Twin Oaks. Two I had slept with and one who hated my guts because at some point during the later part of my time at Twin Oaks I had been shown pornographic pictures of him and his girlfriend that they had posted on the community computer network. Not thinking much of it, I casually mentioned it to someone at a party and it ended up getting really ugly. The truth was, at some point I had become an easy target to hate.

I didn't want to cause any trouble, so I took all my meals away from the community building as to avoid the guy who hated me. It was really good to see Jason again. He had been my healthiest relationship at Twin Oaks, a really sensitive and intelligent human being. He was playful and masculine and a midnight philosopher. He also spoke a little Mandarin Chinese, which was fun because that had been my language focus at school and we could practice a little with each other. He was one of the first enlightened lovers I had and the first guy I stopped having protected sex with.

I remember when we were dating being so attracted to him that I just tried to have sex with him whenever I could. And what was weird to me was that Jason didn't always like that. He wanted every other night off to read in bed and fall asleep to philosophy. I definitely didn't have time for that kind of non-sense.

Jason's body was exactly my type. Broad and strong, but soft around the edges. He confessed to me that he used to be quite a bit heavier, and he carried that on his body in a really good way. He liked to work out to his kettle bell with his shirt off and it would just drive me crazy. He actually told me once that he resented getting sexual attention for his looks from women because he recalled a time when he was heavier, during his sophomore year of college, and feeling ignored by women. I think he silently resented having to be attractive to be noticed.

One thing I noticed during my stay with Jason Shark was how poor, dirty, and ragged everyone seemed to be. I felt like their world was the Wizard of OZ, before OZ, when the movie was still in black and white. I was a bit poor, dirty, and ragged myself, but I had name brand sandals and clean, high quality gear. I never really had any money, but I ate food like Brie and fruit on the regular and enjoyed the occasional $10 breakfast. And all they had was tofu and root vegetables sprinkled with nutritional yeast. Every night for dinner.

Jason hosted me and I stayed with him in his room. The level of filth that he had become conditioned to really blew me away. I remember just feeling like his bed was dirty, that the sheets were so old and worn out and couldn't imagine they had been washed anytime recently. I don't really know why this bothered me so much, but a part of it may be the fact I had crashed on so many couches and stayed with so many different people thus far on my trip- friends and strangers alike-that I had been exposed to how most people lived. Most people had nice things. Nice sheets. Clean blankets. Soap that smelled good.

Our first night together I remember how good it felt to be near his body. We kind of power cuddled and just got reacquainted with each other at first. Jason was the first guy I'd been to bed with since hooking up with James, anf I didn't know what I didn't know until I found out. When the energy turned to sex, I didn't understand consciously what was happening at all. I just remember everything in me protesting when things started to heat up. I withdrew and pushed him away, completely shocked by my reaction. My response startled Jason as well, who was not the kind of guy to ever push for anything without consent. I remember he said kind of firmly,

“Bok Choy, if you don’t want to have sex, just say so.”

It felt almost incomprehensible. Here I was, lying in bed with a totally sexy guy who I really did care about and respect, but I couldn’t sleep with. I didn’t fully know it yet, but I didn’t want to have sex with anyone but James now. He had begun wielding some kind of insane hold over me which had now taken over. What I didn’t know then is that I would find myself in bondage to him in this way for over four years. I would forget what it would feel like to be free from him until after my first date with the man who would later become my husband.

It really was as crazy as it sounds- but after I met my husband, the spiritual bondage to James would be cut immediately. It was such a freeing feeling that I mistook it for love and we rushed into marriage within a matter of months after that infamous first date. And while the story of my marriage could fill its own book, I would soon find myself brutally aware that I had married a man I didn’t know.

Robbie

The second guy at Jason's community that I had history with was Robbie. Robbie was quite a bit older than Jason, probably 15 years, and we had hooked up one time at Twin Oaks in probably one of the most violently unrestrained acts of pure lust and passion of my life thus far. It happened under the influence of a $100 bottle of "post-apocalyptic" brandy, and when I woke in the morning from my drunken stupor, my right shoulder was partially out of socket. This was a semi-regular occurring phenomenon, and I was skilled at reaching over with my left hand and violently pulling my arm until it popped back into place. But usually this happened after throwing my hoop too quickly and forcefully during a throw. Never had it happened during sex.

The morning after our drunken hookup, after popping my shoulder into socket, I sat up in my loft and tried to to remember the details of what had happened. I began to investigate. I followed a trail of Robbies clothes which were shed and it took me right up to his room. Still confused, I knocked on the door and found Robbie, sitting at his computer, completely covered in hickies and bite marks. He looked at me and said "Well, the verdicts out. There's no cure for hickies."

This was unfortunate because, while this incident happened while I was single, after the man with white gloves but before I started dating Jason Shark, Robbie was in a monogamous, pretty serious and committed relationship with a girlfriend he really didn't want to hurt or lose.

I remember being so stunned as I was trying to put together the pieces from last night. I was so drunk that at one point during the actual sex I had blacked out from the alcohol. I figured this out because I remember just having a few drinks with Robbie in his room and then "waking up" to me fucking his brains out up in my loft, but realizing he wasn't wearing a condom. This was super out of the norm for me, because as I mentioned, I didn't start having unprotected sex until Jason and I were in a relationship with each other. And that was in part due to the fact that his sexual practice involved not ejaculating when he climaxed. He was a lover I felt safe with.

As I searched my mind for the details and clues to help me gather my senses around what had happened, I just kept coming back to the moment I "came to," realized we weren't using a condom, and then just freaking out.

I remember Robbie just being super calm, "Don't worry, I won't come inside of you" to me just freaking out even more.

"What the fuck is your problem? My sister got pregnant from pre-come!" Which was true, but somehow guys just seem to forget is very possible.

The night came to me in flashes, and I wasn't quite sure of the chronological order of every detail. But definitely one moment was seared in my mind because it had felt so deliciously dirty. I remember when I was starting to give him a blow-job, he just whispered to me "Good Girl" and I just thought that was hilarious.

I kept our hookup a secret for a long time, but did tell my best friend right away every detail I could remember. She appreciated the "Good Girl" moment as much as I did, and we started an inside joke where periodically, if either one of us did something well, we would say to the other "Good Girl" and just laugh.

The really fun thing about my best friend was making fun of all the guys we were sleeping with with each other. She had a real thing for beautiful men, which meant a lot of them were lacking in intellect and self-awareness and we had such a lovely secret world where we were queens and all the guys were just our little joke.

But aside from our solitary sexual exploit, Robbie and I just had an ongoing flirtation but nothing serious. He was very intellectually sexy and he knew how to leverage that to sleep with almost any woman he wanted. I later found out that he and Jason Shark were constantly competing with other for the same women at this small community. It made sense to me. They both had similar body types and were richly intelligent. Robbie was more cunning and Jason was more youthful.

Cross-Check vs. Long Haul Trucker

(*) *Let me level with you about Robbie vs. Jason and what bikes they are. Because they are both very similar with notable distinctions. Both are a chromoly, smooth riding steel. If you know anything about Surleys, Jason is a Cross-Check and Robbie is a Long-Haul Trucker. And by that I mean that they have similar geometries, builds, and riders. Cross-checks make for a more spirited bike. Long-Haul Truckers carry more mass and can take more abuse over the long haul. In the end, both excellent options that no one with a huge boner for steel bikes would regret.*

I was staying with Jason and spent my nights sleeping in his bed with him, but like I mentioned we weren't having sex. I remember being kind of excited to see Robbie, and recall a "date" where we met up on the trampoline. We talked and flirted and I remember showing him my legs with pride, with all their bruises and grease stains and bulging muscles, and I asked him if he thought they looked tough. I had never been as strong as I was now, and my muscle power was exciting me. I remember what Robbie replied.

"Tough isn't the word I would use. Because to me, tough implies abuse. To me, your legs are powerful." I loved that.

I remember we kissed, and it was overdue and really nice. But nothing materialized beyond that. I later asked him why he didn't hit on me when I was visiting, and he said it was for a variety of reasons. He didn't know what was up with me and Jason, he was friends with the guy who still hated my guts, and apparently he said that on the trampoline I was going on and on about "Some biker guy who was really hot." I must have been telling him about James without realizing that that was a slight turn off for him. In the end, I think he was just picking up on the fact that I didn't want to sleep with him even though I didn't know it at the time. Fucking James.

After about a week of this relatively nice R&R, it was time to leave Kansas and get back on the road. The wedding was approaching. Jason drove me into town and I told him I wanted to stop at a McDonalds. He was amused at how I was eating, and as a philosopher on a self-sufficient and organic vegan vegetable farm, it was a really big step for him to eat a McDouble and "factory-farmed" meat. As we parted, for the last time we would ever see each other, Jason thanked me for helping him have the experience he did of eating that meat. I didn't really understand what was going on for him during our meal, but I was happy I was of help to him. I headed out with my ukulele and rubber Skello-Kitty strapped to my back rack. I was back on the road

Kiss [10]

Waking in my tent, it is too hot even to move to dress myself. Too scared to get out naked, I just lie and strum my ukulele, waiting for motivation. Eventually though, clothed in my black catsuit, I kneel before my tree-bush toward tiny crisp mocha brown leaves.

This Kiss.

Quick and playful.

The Kind Rancher

After leaving the community with Jason Shark and Robbie, I was only about 10 days out until the wedding was to commence in the mountains of Boone, North Carolina. I didn't fully understand it at the time, but I was not completely recovered from the Pneumonia. I had difficulty breathing deeply and I was having weak and dizzy spells. One day, at a gas station in the middle of nowhere, I ordered a hot dog and just rested my head down. I couldn't move. And so I just gave in to the overwhelming impulse to rest.

A friendly rancher was in the store, had seen my bicycle out front, and noticed a weary and wayward traveler with a twinge of compassion. Because of my sex and age, I seemed to generate a lot of compassion from men who were old enough to be my father and who had young adult children of their own. Especially men with daughters. He approached me and asked me if I was OK. I confessed everything. About how I still needed to get to Boone, North Carolina and how all I wanted to do was rest in a hot bath and sleep in a warm bed.

He invited me to rest on his horse ranch, and told me he would help make sure I arrived at the wedding in time. I sensed both his gentleness and genuineness and immediately took him up on his offer. After loading up my bike, which was over 90 pounds now, he took me up a winding mountainside in his truck to his horse ranch. He let me in the house, and instructed me to take a long bath and rest on the bed in the guest room until dinner. He told me after dinner everyone helped with the horse chores, because there were over seventy horses. I told him I would be happy to help.

I soaked in a large, clawfoot tub and used shampoo and conditioner that had a picture of a horses mane on it. I was amused that everything seemed to revolve around horses here. I fell asleep in a clean and tidy room under a lovely and warm hand made quilt. It felt wonderful to sleep warm and clean. At 6pm a small and infeebled woman knocked on my door and invited me to supper. She was the rancher's mother who lived with them and had dementia. I was joined at the table by the ranchers high school age daughter who was lovely and delightful.

On the menu my first night was "smorgasbord" as the rancher's mother called it, and she simply just pulled out everything from the fridge and placed it on the table. It was great eating for me, as I love the way farmers eat. The grandmother told us all that as a little girl, "smorgasbord night" was always her favorite. And then she seemed for forget that that she had said that, and kept informing us all of this fact. Finally, the rancher's daughter said

"We know grandma, you've told us four times now" to which the grandmother expressed her deep embarrassment over her dementia. The daughter immediatly exclaimed "I'm sorry grandma!" This family was so loving and sweet to each other. I loved every minute with them.

When it was time for horse chores, I was put in charge of "pushing the ponies" as I ended up calling it. The rancher and daughter would just point to a horse and my job was to push it on its butt until it walked into the barn to be fed, watered, and quickly brushed. Because there were 70 horses, it took several hours. But it was such a lovely time, everyone together and cooperating.

The favorite horse at the ranch was a young foul named "Button" who just could do no harm in the eyes of the rancher and his daughter. Sometimes at breakfast the daughter would spot Button just walking around the front yard of the house and exclaim, excitedly "Look at Button!" like this was the most exciting event of the year.

As I said, I loved every minute I spent with the kind rancher and his family. I rested and helped for 5 days until finally it was either time for me to get on the road or find a ride. The rancher told me he wanted to help me any way he could. In the end he volunteered to drive me all the way up the mountain into Boone, NC directly to the hotel reserved for guests of the wedding. When we finally decided to leave, he said to me

"I hate to ask you this, but could give me gas money to drive you there?" I had enough left from my cash gig in DC and said "Absolutley, no problem."

During the drive he told me about his financial problems on the ranch, and about how someone who had agreed to pay him $50,000 for something simply didn't pay him. I just listened and then decided to treat him to lunch when we stopped. We both ordered side salads with our meal, which was novel for me because at this point in my ride, food was measured by it caloric density and calorie-to-dollar value. McDonald's and Hersheys were the clear winners. A salad felt almost senseless.

As we drove up the winding mountain to the resort, it almost felt like a modern day Odyssey filled with challenges and almost impossible obstacles which we had to overcome in order to successfully arrive on time. Somehow, it all worked out and the rancher helped me wheel my bicycle toward a hotel room occupied by my brother and his wife. I didn't really know what had been happening behing the scenes among the men in my family, but my father was upset with me and told my brother why. When I arrived at his room, my brother started screaming at me, telling me that I had "fucked my dad over" and how he wasn't going to let me stay in the room reserved for me and my sister. I started crying because I was so sensitive to this unbridled rage directed toward me with no warning. And I felt ashamed that my kind rancher friend was seeing how my family treated me.

I had plenty of cash to rent my own room. When I went to the lobby, I befriended the teller and I commented that I felt like some of the flower arrangements were not expressing their true potential. She agreed and together we worked on them and the lobby really opened up with a fresh and rich energy. I tucked this experience away in my mind, and promised to remind myself at a later time how thrilling flower arranging can be and to pursue it further when the opportunity presented itself again.

When my sister found me and met me in my room, she saw me in a skin tight black "catsuit" with bleach blonde hair and eyebrows. My hair had this great kind of flapper girl natural wave to it and I was very happy with it. She told me that she felt like I looked like a superhero. I was so pleased by this compliment. I was very happy with my body at this point. I was incredibly muscular and toned. I remember we hung out in the kitchen at the resort and I was drinking beer and wearing a vintage blue-slip I bought at the same antique clothing store I bought my evening gown and pearls. And my sister just seemed intoxicated around me, but not because of the beer. She later told me she was on a high delighting in my power.

At the wedding, I looked amazing and seemed to shock everyone in my family with the fact that I had made it considering what they were hearing. My dad's narrative to the family was that I was an out of control homeless person who was living on the streets with a mental illness that was the result of demonic possesssion that I hadn't been freed from because my dad hadn't laid his hands upon me. I remember sitting with my cousins, aunt, and brother as they were having a kind of "intervention" with me.

In my family's paradigm, there were things a good Christian did. They went to church and they worked a full time job if they were not in school. No matter what you were working- either in your job or more for God. Ideally, both in the form of full-time ministry, which was my father's and several uncle's backgrounds. It was the Protestant work ethic on steroids. They studied the Bible and always deferred their understanding to "The Word"- which was never to be challenged under the lens of patriarchy or feminist theory. Just the word "Feminism" was a bad word, let alone theory to operate under. As a female, you presented a certain way. Purity and Chastity. Ideally, you wanted to marry young, start a family and homeschool your offspring. But if you varied from that ideal, you worked and went to church. Because if you were doing that, somehow you were doing enough. Anything that differed was met with judgement, anxiety, and reproach.

They were asking what I was doing to get well, I explained that I needed a ride and $1300 to get to a very special clinic called the Pfeiffer Treatment Center. Eventually, James would give me a ride and $1300 and take me to this clinic where my illness would be treated with specific nutrition and compounded supplements and histamine blockers. This actually worked great until they ran out of money and had to close suddenly. As I explained the potential this clinic had to offer me, my cousin kept saying over and over "Jenell, you don't need the the Pfeiffer Treatment Center. You need Jesus"

I was so exhausted of my illness being moralized and then judged by my insane and conservative evangelical family. I finally got up and drank excessively in rebellion to this confrontation that felt somewhere between an outright assault and a formal reprimand. I licked frosting off of cupcakes and danced with my lovely and beautiful cousins who radiated a freedom in their youth and femininity that was as intoxicating to be around as all the wine.

In the morning I was incredibly sick and I was in denial that it was entirely alcohol related. I thought I had the stomach flu and that I must have picked it up because my immune system was still suppressed from the pneumonia.

Kiss [11]

Vomiting up orange juice in the Ridge Hotel, high up in the mountains of Boone, NC, all I can do is kiss the tile beside the toilet, swearing this time I'd had my last drink. Swearing this time, I'd remember this feeling.

The Kiss.

White and smooth and cold.

Part 5
New Beginnings

When my bike ride was finished, my life completely transformed in ways I never could have anticipated or imagined. I found a wonderful place to live and actually got a job at that really cool bike shop with a cat. I would finally graduate college with my B.A. in mathematics, get married, and conceive a child by my 29th birthday. My experience being pregnant was extremely profound and healing in a way nothing before could compare to.

The intimacy and bond I felt with my baby while he was growing and developing was rich beyond description. I remember one night meditating on the fact that before he would come to know my face, my baby boy will have known the beating of my heart. How I fully loved him and was completely willing to give up my entire body for him before I knew anything else about him or who he would become. My relationship with my son is how God spoke to me during this time in my life.

I remember so clearly my labor and what an incredible gift that experience was. How my crown opened up entirely and connected directly to God, who fully equipped me with all the grace and strength to bring my baby into the world with no medical interventions. There is no way of understanding my labor and delivery other than supernatural. For how could I have known how to birth? It was a full on download from heaven.

After delivery, when they placed him on my chest, I realized I'd never waited so long for something so exciting as meeting my sweet baby. And I thought maybe this is how God felt about his children. Waiting and wanting to meet them with. To see birth and rebirth. To hold in awe and love.

I also remembered how reflecting on my bike ride reshaped my self perception. How I stopped seeing myself as deficient because I had mental health challenges. Rather, I felt strong in my resolve and resourcefulness.

How I learned to trust not just in myself, but in my ability to receive support from others and supernatural provision from God. How, looking back, I wasn't chasing Jesus on my ride but Jesus was chasing me. Showing His goodness with every kindness in his body. And how a living and dynamic body which showed love was always His greatest dream.

It would come to me in a vision, but the supremacy of Christ's message of Love would be revealed to me in a way that I could receive and then never doubt again. It didn't come from academic study and rigid guidelines. Rather, it came as direct revelation with a richness I always knew was lacking from the evangelical persuasion. I carried the lessons and revelations from my ride tenderly in my spirit.

Like when I was biking in the sweltering sun on an Illinois highway with semis whizzing past me with no shoulder with a broken spoke and chain grease dripping down my calves. I recall, in that moment, finding within myself everything I needed to keep going. My mantra became "All that I have is all that I need. All that I need is all that I have" and how I didn't fully understand all the power of this awakening until years later.

How once I opened myself to the free grace and abundance of guidance, support and love from everyone supporting humanity's progressions toward greater and greater Love consciousness I never truly lacked for anything. Visions came to me from Jesus when I needed to feel safe enough to forgive. Wisdom from the Tao de Ching teaching me to "hold my high side with my low side, because then I can hold the whole world." Then revelation from above offering me support and wisdom which felt so safe and right in my intuition which would later open up to me and compel me to know that I can always consult my inner knowing to understand truth and love. How my gratitude meditation practice shifted when I stopped being grateful for what was outside of me and became aware that I was grateful for what was within.

That I can always choose love in any moment. And when I can't find it I can simply ask for help. That if you truly want to expand your heart center toward greater and greater Love consciousness, there will always be help and assistance along the way. That Love never meets you, who you are and anything you have done, with shame or humiliation or judgment. How the evangelical western Christian church has totally missed the mark with their obsession around shame, judgment, morality, and intellectual academic study. We all have permission to experience and embrace what we truly know about The Way in own way, on own terms, and with a community of our choosing.

If you are reading this, in a way you are now a part of this community to me. I needed to write the story, 15 years after the fact, in order to stand in the strength of telling my story entirely from my own perspective while allowing myself to see my humanity- in all its fragility and contradiction- aiming to please no one but myself. The journey of this writing project was incredibly healing for me personally, but my hope is that somehow, in whatever small way it may have, it might inspire its reader to tell their own story and see it in a new light. That your own journey of experiencing the tragedy in the brokenness of your humanity and then the redemption found in discovering a love that is everywhere and in everything. A journey both unique and deeply personal yet entirely universal.

I hope that maybe you may find your spirit so filled with gratitude that you have been granted yet another breath and another sunrise that you too may consider Rumi's invitation to kneel before the earth and humbly kiss it. To learn the lesson that the shasta daisy has come to teach us- that even your own small and quiet deeds contribute to universal life goodness.

Thank you for sharing my journey with me. I'm sending you love and light from a small town in central Iowa filled with bunnies where I sleep warm and safe each night and kiss the forehead of a little boy who dreams of legos and treehouses.

I wish wonderful things for you. You are a radiant light made from the cosmos and endowed with the gift of consciousness which has no end and no limit. Heaven dreamed you and your very existence is the radiant joy of the author of everything in the universe.

If you could see that as much I do, I know every wound in your heart could heal in an instant. And even if you don't see it or believe it, you could ask for help to see the truth about yourself clearly. And help will always arrive. That even the smallest act of faith is never lost or wasted. Thank you for your time and spending it with me. You have given me such a gift and I feeled compelled to give back to you anyway I can. Please, do not hesitate to reach out to me if there is anything I can offer to support you. You can email me anytime at jenell.nyberg@gmail.com.

Thank you again.

Sincerely Yours,

Jenell Nyberg

aka

Bok Choy

Made in the USA
Monee, IL
21 May 2024

58589984R00075